The Unfought Battle

The
Unfought Battle

JON KIMCHE

Stein and Day / *Publishers* / New York

First published in the United States of America
by Stein and Day/Publishers 1968
Copyright © 1968 by Jon Kimche
Library of Congress Catalog Card No. 67–25619
All rights reserved
Printed in England
Stein and Day/*Publishers*/7 East 48 Street, New York, N.Y. 10017

To Basil Liddell Hart

who made me understand the importance
of dissent – even from his own views

Contents

Contents

INTRODUCTION

The Silent Historians

It is common ground among surviving British and German generals that the Germans lost the second world war because they committed themselves to certain decisive battles from which they should have withdrawn.

It is the thesis of this book, however, that in the course of the entire war, in all theatres, the most decisive and the most costly of all battles was the one to which Britain and France would not commit themselves – the 'unfought battle' during the first three weeks of September 1939.

It cost more lives than all other battles taken together – at least twenty million. This unfought battle has been virtually ignored by the historians of the war, unmentioned by the politicians, and explained away by the generals. Many of the most relevant facts in the official histories, and in the files of the Allied cabinets, have been evidently withheld; some were deliberately falsified before presentation to the cabinets concerned with the decision-making in the summer of 1939.

The basic facts of the unfought battle were that during the second week of September 1939, while the war in Poland was still undecided, the German troops in the unfinished Siegfried Line on the western front totalled eight undermanned first-line divisions and twenty-five undermanned territorial, home-guard and reserve divisions, a total of thirty-three mostly ill-trained and incompletely equipped units which could hardly be described as anything more than a scratch home-defence force.

The French had eighty-five divisions assembled in the west when their mobilization was completed (there is some difference of opinion and accounting on this subject but even the lowest figure given is seventy-two divisions in the west).

Moreover, a considerable part of the German troops were new recruits; many had never fired live ammunition; and their total supply of ammunition was calculated to last for barely three days of war. The Siegfried Line was unfinished and in part unusable for active defence. German intelligence reports – and those prepared at the time by the Chief of German Intelligence on the western front, General Liss – show that the Germans were dangerously exposed in the west. General Westphal, a divisional staff officer in the Siegfried Line at the time, was convinced that if the allies had attacked early in September, they would have reached the Rhine with little trouble, and would probably have crossed it without serious opposition. But there is no evidence that the possibility of such an attack had been considered by either the British or French General Staff, or by their governments.

Both governments blamed pacifist public opinion and the lack of will to fight in the French and British armies. This book will show that this was not true; that, on the contrary, there was great pressure to bring about a decisive battle but that it was the political and military leaders who did not believe in it (or in themselves?).

The material I have collected reveals, in my opinion, the need for a fundamental reconsideration of existing techniques and practices of diplomatic and intelligence reporting. In particular, it raises doubts about the value of diplomatic missions as we have come to know them as adequate channels of information for their respective governments.

It may be that the transmission of accurate information has become too complex politically for it to be left to diplomats and most not-so-secret agents. The country which will have the courage to break first with the outmoded patterns of diplomacy and espionage will not only gain considerable immediate advantage and save vast sums of money; but it will also pioneer the new understanding of international relations without which nations will continue unnecessarily to fear and suspect each other and, on occasion, fail to recognize the real dangers that may threaten them.

1

Three Legends

The week which began on 7 March 1939 and ended with the *dénouement* of 15 March must rank as one of the strangest – and most revealing – in the modern history of man. It has been recorded with greater detail and more apologetics than any other similar period; and yet, as we retrace our steps over what looks like familiar ground, with all the added advantage of official, personal and hitherto secret documentation, we are faced suddenly by one stark and irrefutable fact: the contemporary landscape of that fateful week of March was drawn by men who were quite ignorant of its actual contours.

In every case, in that of the English and of the Germans, of the French and the Russians, the Poles and the Swiss, the diplomatic service and the secret intelligence service failed to provide the detailed, specific and, above all, accurate information on which their governments had to base their decisions and their actions. If the opening of the archives of the immediate pre-war years has revealed anything, it is the absolute failure of both the diplomatic system and that of the secret service in gathering *and communicating* information.

It was the breakdown of this system which, in the final analysis, made possible the last great war – because without accurate and detailed information there can be no effective prevention of war.

There is another and possibly even more dangerous side to this failure to provide reliable information, for its place, as we shall see, is taken by fear – mutual fear – and exaggeration. These were the central features of the crises which preceded the outbreak of war in 1939. And yet, precise and accurate information could have been made available to the diplomats and secret services of the Powers principally concerned as never before – or since – in their history. For it was there, somewhere in the pipeline, and we shall have to ask ourselves how it was that it failed to reach its destination.

What we seek, therefore, is something even more far-reaching than answers to our initial two questions, whether a military defeat of Hitler's Germany was possible during the first weeks of the war in September 1939; and if it was possible, what prevented it from happening.

Before we return, however, to our crucial week of March, we may consider with advantage the curious complex fear which had haunted the British and French governments – and their supporting circles – during the Munich crisis. It was, as we now know, not the decisive element in the Munich settlement, but it provides an instructive example of how governmental opinion and judgement was shaped.

Three letters from Tom Jones, the *éminence grise* on the fringe of the Chamberlain government and *The Times*, and at the heart of the *Observer* and the Astors' 'Cliveden' circle, throw more light on the mood of those days than does a volume of selected documents.

On 23 September 1938, Jones wrote to his close friend Abraham Flexner, Director of the Institute for Advanced Study at Princeton University,[1] that the British had not faced the possibility of war because the French Ministers had 'besought ours to avoid it at all costs. They could put only 700 planes in the air!' Moreover, the British Ministers responsible for air defence, Sir Samuel Hoare and Kingsley Wood, 'knew that London was at Germany's mercy'. Jones added that no one in London 'seemed able to state with any certainty what Russia was prepared to do, or what the result of the slaughter of the

[1] Thomas Jones, *A Diary with Letters, 1931–1950*, p. 409.

generals would be'. He concluded that they were all filled with gloom and shame and wondered whether there was anything they could still rescue 'from the débâcle'.

Two days later, Jones was again writing to Flexner, on the eve of the Munich conference, that at the back of all the talk and the newspapers, of the alarms and excursions, was 'the fear in the heart of Ministers in London and Paris'. The small-scale experience of Spain had been enough to make them dread the fate of their great city populations. Lord Brand had shown him a letter, Jones continued, which Lindbergh[2] had written the previous week: 'he says that the air power of Germany is greater than that of all the European nations combined and that they could not be prevented by us or by France from laying the great capitals level with the ground.'

And four days later, on 29 September, the day of Munich, Tom Jones returns to the subject in a third and rather more revealing letter to a close friend. He had himself spoken to Lindbergh and the experience had left its mark. 'Since my talk with Lindbergh on Monday,' he writes to Gwendoline Davies, 'I've sided with those working for peace at any cost in humiliation, because of the picture of our relative unpreparedness in the air and on the ground which Lindbergh painted, and because of his belief that the democracies would be crushed absolutely and finally.'

He goes on to describe how Arthur Salter, a leading Liberal and outstanding League of Nations man, had come round to his view that they ought to tell the Czechs plainly that nothing that Britain could do would save them from destruction, and how he (Tom Jones) had put everything he had learnt from authoritative people to Stanley Baldwin and impressed on him that he 'by speaking in the Lords today – as originally arranged – could save the country from war'. Baldwin was 'for peace at any price'.

---

[2] Lindbergh, Colonel Charles, a popular and likeable American, the first man to fly solo across the Atlantic, who was intent on impressing the British and French with the 'overwhelming superiority' of the Luftwaffe – and succeeded far more effectively than did the German propagandists.

Jones had then borrowed one of the Astor cars and sent Lindbergh to see Lloyd George at Churt 'so that he might learn at first hand what an air expert thought of our chances'.[3]

And to round off the picture, Jones wrote a fourth letter to Lady Grigg, describing the information which the Services had provided for the Prime Minister as basis for his stand at Munich. The Navy would be ready for war in a year's time; and the Army and Air Force by the end of 1941. As to the French, Jones opined that 'had the French Parliament been summoned, not more than ten Senators would have voted for war. Had the Government left Paris when the bombing began, the chances were high that a Communist provisional government would be set up in Paris. The French peasant was willing to fight on the defensive, but not to undertake an offensive against the Siegfried Line.'

These were not isolated or extremist views. They were shared by the Air Staff, their collective view was designed to support Lindbergh's gloomy foreboding and the political conclusions which the Chamberlain government drew from it. Sholto Douglas, the then Assistant Chief of the Air Staff, recalls his own reactions and those of his colleagues of the Air Staff.[4] They could not understand 'those who would have had us risk a fight with Germany at the time of Munich'. The harsh facts of the RAF's inferior strength made him 'feel a steadily mounting alarm as the political negotiations proceeded during those weeks of the summer of 1938'. He was certain that Britain, and especially London, 'would be in for a terrible and probably disastrous pasting from the German air force'. In a mood of desperation he put his views to Sir Cyril Newall, his chief, who authorized him to place them before the Air Staff. They became the basis of an appreciation which was prepared for the Minister, Sir Kingsley Wood, who in turn passed it to the Cabinet. 'It was with this vital information in mind that Chamberlain had to conduct himself in the tortuous nego-

[3] Jones, p. 411.

[4] Sholto Douglas, *Memoirs*, vol. II, *Years of Command*, pp. 37, 39.

tiations that ended at Munich,' Sholto Douglas reminds us.[5]

Baldwin, Lindbergh and the Air Staff; it was no mean burden that Chamberlain carried with him to Munich. They had impressed on him what he had expected to hear from them: the first of the legends – Germany's superior preparedness for war on land and in the air.

It was, moreover, the culmination of a series of reports prepared by the British Chiefs of Staff for the Committee of Imperial Defence, to the effect that Britain was unready for war; her armed forces and industry required more time to rearm, and that the French were not prepared to conduct an offensive against Germany either on land or in the air.

The French had also received the Lindbergh treatment. The Air Force commander, General Vuillemin, was so paralysed by his information that he had informed Daladier, the French Prime Minister, on the eve of his departure for the Munich conference, that after the first days of war France would be left without an air force. At Munich, Goering's spokesman, General Bodenschatz, took Paul Stehlin,[6] the French assistant air attaché (who was also the agent of the *Deuxième Bureau*) aside and told him that the Luftwaffe was at that moment ready to launch a blitz-like (he loved that word) attack against Czechoslovakia. Two thousand strike aircraft were assembled near the Czech border. For weeks they had been prepared for this action. Their bombs were loaded. Their targets settled. The pilots were practised in every detail of their mission. They were prepared to accept and replace losses up to fifty per cent, but all set targets would be destroyed in the process.

Stehlin passed Bodenschatz's confidence to the French delegation and noted after the Munich agreement[7] that there had been no need for the Luftwaffe to go into action. Its mere

[5] ibid., pp. 44–5.

[6] Stehlin has given a full and very frank account of his mission in his book *Témoignage pour l'Histoire*, and in a somewhat shortened German edition *Auftrag in Berlin*. See p. 124, German edition. Unless otherwise indicated, reference is made to the German edition.

[7] Stehlin, p. 128.

threat sufficed to keep Europe on tenterhooks, and, one might say, constituted the decisive element in Germany's diplomatic victories. It enabled her to win her conquests without recourse to war. They had every reason to be content with the Luftwaffe as an instrument of German policy.

But the Nazi leaders, at that time, had quite a different set of preoccupations. They were not thinking of bombing either London or Paris. They were concerned with averting a disaster nearer home. The High Command of the armed forces was divided and, in part, avowedly disloyal to Hitler. Some were planning his arrest and overthrow; others sought to ensure that Germany did not get involved in a war with either France or Britain. The situation report which the Wehrmacht's chief of operations, General Jodl, gave at the Nuremberg Trials needs to be measured against these earlier British and French assessments of the situation. Jodl was asked by his counsel, Dr Exner, on 4 June 1946, whether he had believed that Germany's conflict with Czechoslovakia could be localized.

Jodl replied[8] that he was convinced of this. 'I could not imagine that the Fuehrer, in the position we were in, would start a conflict with Britain and France which would lead to our immediate collapse.'

He had discussed this aspect with General Stuelpnagel on 8 September 1938 when the General had come to him worried over the possibility that Hitler might depart from his previously defined position and allow himself to be 'dragged into military action in spite of the danger of French intervention'. Jodl had shared this concern with Stuelpnagel. He was worried by the weakness of the German position. 'It was out of the question,' Jodl explained to the Court, 'to hold out against a hundred French divisions with only five fighting divisions and seven reserve divisions in the western fortifications which were nothing but a large construction site. This was militarily impossible,' Jodl added for good measure.[9]

[8] *Trial of Major War Criminals*, vol. XV, p. 361.
[9] ibid., p. 361.

This view was shared by Fabian von Schlabrendorff,[10] one of the principal survivors of the attempts to displace Hitler. Schlabrendorff was convinced that there was no risk involved in an uncompromising stand by the Western Powers during the summer of 1938. It had become clear during the German occupation of Austria in March 1938, he claims, that the German Army was in no shape to fight a major war that year, 'especially if such a war meant military engagements on several fronts'. It was von Schlabrendorff's considered opinion that even an attack against Czechoslovakia alone would have presented serious difficulties for the Germans; they still lacked the necessary arms and equipment for a break through the Czech frontier fortifications.

'Had England and France come into the war while the Germans were engaged in fighting the Czechs, there can be no doubt that the defeat of Germany would have followed in short order.' Schlabrendorff is convinced that the British Secret Service was fully informed of this situation and he cannot believe that Chamberlain and the government did not share this knowledge.

General von Manstein, who had not been associated with the movement to get rid of Hitler, later confirmed this military reading of the situation. He told the Nuremberg Court (on 9 August 1946)[11] that if war had broken out in 1938 the Germans could not have effectively defended either 'our western border or our Polish frontier'. He had no doubts whatsoever that 'had Czechoslovakia defended herself, we would have been held up by her fortifications, for we did not have the means to break through'. And Hitler himself, when he later inspected the Czech defence system, conceded that the German armies would have run into serious danger, and that he now understood why his Generals had urged restraint.[12] But, unlike his generals, Hitler understood the mentality of his principal opponents in London and Paris.

[10] F. von Schlabrendorff, *Secret War Against Hitler*, p. 88.
[11] *Trial of Major War Criminals*, vol. XX, p. 606.
[12] Pertinax, *Grave-diggers of France*, p. 5.

The British Foreign Secretary, Lord Halifax, told his friend, the Dean of Westminster, that he had never read *Mein Kampf*; moreover, he made no secret of his intention, when he became Foreign Secretary, after Eden's resignation in February 1938, to make every effort 'short of overstepping the frontiers of honour to avert a war'[13] which he was convinced at the time Great Britain was certain to lose. In the months between Munich and the fateful week in March, Halifax repeatedly dwelt, in his correspondence with his ambassadors, on the consequences for British foreign policy of having inadequate armed strength to sustain a firm policy. On 1 November 1939, he told his ambassador in Paris, Sir Eric Phipps, that 'henceforth we must count with German predominance in Central Europe'. It was an accurate reflection of the government's outlook immediately after Munich. At heart, they still believed that peace was possible, and they reassured themselves – and the country – by a controlled measure of rearmament.

The key for this lay in the dual character of British rearmament. Its purpose was strictly defensive; a reinsurance just in case the government's anticipations of the peaceful intentions of future German policy towards the British were mistaken. It was neither designed nor intended – either before or after Munich – to present a challenge to Germany's dominant position in Central Europe, no matter what happened. Even more to the point of our inquiry is to see whether there was any measurable change in this outlook after the German occupation of Czechoslovakia.

This brings us again to that week in March 1939, when all this fear, ignorance, misinformation and concern for the preservation of peace 'at any cost', culminated in a series of seemingly unrelated events that were to set the stage – despite all previous intentions to the contrary – for the confrontation and challenge of Germany. As the week began, there appeared no sense of foreboding in the Cabinet. The Secretary for War, Leslie Hore-Belisha, was putting the finishing touches to the

[13] The Earl of Birkenhead, *The Life of Lord Halifax*, p. 419.

Army Estimates which he was about to present to Parliament on Wednesday, 8 March, and in which the word 'Germany' was not mentioned. Sir Samuel Hoare, the Home Secretary, was also preparing a speech, for Friday's (10 March) annual gathering of his constituents in Chelsea. He wanted to make some reference to the marked improvement in international relations and consulted the Prime Minister about this. Chamberlain told Hoare to discourage the view that war was inevitable and to insist upon the great possibilities of peace.[14]

The Prime Minister himself arranged a confidential briefing of the press on the Thursday, the day before Hoare was to make his reassuring speech in Chelsea. Chamberlain advised the lobby correspondents that Europe was at last 'settling down to a period of tranquillity',[15] and there were good prospects for an early disarmament agreement. Hoare's flight of language was somewhat more extravagant. He saw a vision of the great leaders of Europe, Stalin and Hitler, Mussolini and Chamberlain, and the Frenchman Daladier, coming together and providing the basis 'for a new golden age of peace'. For good measure he denounced the 'jitterbugs' who feared the prospect of war. It is evident now that neither Chamberlain nor Hoare was intent on misleading the general public; they believed that what they were saying was correct. The Cabinet had no anticipation of trouble.[16] The Prime Minister departed after his reassuring press

[14] Viscount Templewood, *Nine Troubled Years*, p. 328.

[15] 'Arms Pact May be Signed after Parley in Summer' was the *Daily Express*'s hopeful headline across its front page on Friday. *The Times* also gave great prominence to the 'Improvement in International Outlook' that morning.

[16] Templewood, p. 328; see also Feiling, *The Life of Neville Chamberlain*, p. 396. On 19 February, Chamberlain had written to his sister: 'All the information I get seems to point in the direction of peace.' Three days later, speaking in Blackburn, he said that trade had improved after the German Chancellor's speech in which he gave expression to his hope for peace and the speedy end of the war in Spain. Chamberlain added that there were also 'other indications' which encouraged him to think that this trade improvement would develop further in 1939 'unhampered by political anxieties'. He agreed 'with Herr Hitler' that cooperation between their two peoples in full confidence would be fortunate for the whole world; he would go even further and say that 'nothing would conduce more greatly to the establishment of world peace'.

conference for a long weekend of fishing; the Foreign Secretary went to his retreat in Oxford, and the press took up the cue given to it by the men-in-the-know in Whitehall. The papers welcomed the new mood and saw in the impending visit to Germany of the President of the Board of Trade, Oliver Stanley, yet another step on the way of settling the outstanding differences in Europe.

In fact, Sir Alexander Cadogan, the Permanent Under-Secretary at the Foreign Office, had just received a reassuring personal letter from Sir Neville Henderson, the British Ambassador in Berlin, written on 9 March, together with a highly confidential review of Anglo-German relations. Henderson noted in his letter that he was still hearing 'wild stories of attacks in various directions, but I frankly don't believe a word of them. So long as we go quietly on with our defence preparations all will, in my opinion, be well. I believe the Germans want peace very badly ...' The Foreign Secretary replied at once with a personal letter after his return from the Oxford weekend. Writing on Monday, 13 March, Halifax noted that he, too, felt that there had been 'a negative improvement', rumours and scares had died down; he did not have the impression that 'the German Government are planning mischief in any particular quarter.' He hoped, though, he added lightly in parentheses, that they were not 'even as I write' taking 'an unhealthy interest in the Slovak situation'.

It was a curiously relaxed reply considering that on the Saturday, 11 March, two days earlier, after the press had reported the hopeful turn in affairs and the morning after Hoare's reassuring speech in Chelsea, the senior Intelligence Officer at the Foreign Office brought disturbing information to Sir Alexander Cadogan (the Permanent Under-Secretary). He informed Cadogan that reliable intelligence had reached him that the Germans proposed to occupy Czechoslovakia 'within the next 24 hours'.[17] Sir Alexander noted the information, but appeared neither convinced nor shaken by the imminence of the

[17] Ian Colvin, *Vansittart in Office*, p. 290, quoting from Sir Alexander Cadogan's unpublished private diary.

threat. He advised the Foreign Secretary but appeared also to have communicated to him his own doubts, for Halifax decided to take no action and to proceed with his weekend plans. Chamberlain was similarly told and likewise decided not to let such unlikely news disturb his fishing weekend. There is no evidence of any anticipatory alarm by the Chiefs of the Imperial General Staff or by the French. When the Germans occupied Prague on 15 March, they were surprised. They had not expected it. The machinery of diplomatic and intelligence communication had somehow failed to function. Admittedly, there had been no lack of anticipatory rumblings and actual warnings, but these had either not reached the right persons or they were not believed.[18]

The question here again – as later – is to establish clearly the source of the error. The information did reach the Foreign Office.[19] We know this from Cadogan's private diary. Why was it not checked; why were no precautionary measures taken; why did Chamberlain and Halifax not give it a second thought? After all, this was six months after Munich. It is difficult to avoid the conclusion that not only Chamberlain and Halifax, but all the Cabinet and most of the Service Chiefs, did not want to believe the information about the impending destruction of Czechoslovakia and the Munich settlement. The records allow no other conclusion; and much the same applies, too, to the situation in France. The French were, if anything, more accurately informed by their embassy in Berlin. They were given no excuse for remaining in the dark about Hitler's intentions. But, like their British colleagues, they refused to believe.

This was reflected in a leading article in *The Times*, forty-eight hours after the Secret Service had warned Sir Alexander Cadogan at the Foreign Office that the Germans were about to march. 'If anything distinguishes this year from its predecessor,' wrote *The Times* on Monday morning, 13 March, 'it is the knowledge that Germany has completed those demands upon

18 See Stehlin, pp. 186, 198–9; also Colvin, p. 204.
19 It also reached the French authorities – see Stehlin, pp. 162–3.

her neighbours which by their own professions, they were unable conscientiously to contest, and yet failed to satisfy while the way of orderly settlement was still open.' The Munich settlement had been tragic but just. There had been no justification for going to war against Germany. That was the basis of the government's willingness to negotiate. 'War was not held off in September,' *The Times* explained, 'either by lack of military resources or by an unworthy reluctance on the part of the Government.' This, it said, was quite incorrect, and it was equally false to suggest, either at home or abroad, that the rapid progress of rearmament was reshaping British aims. They were prepared, now as then, to negotiate, and the paper called on the British government for a 'broader statement' of its peace policy which would make it a rallying ground for all people of goodwill.[20]

The Times was not alone in its hopeful approach to the Ides of March. The British Ambassador in Berlin had returned to his post in mid-February after a 'serious illness', about the genuineness of which he was at pains to reassure Ribbentrop. He wanted the Germans to understand that his illness had not been a diplomatic device to express Britain's distaste of the anti-Jewish pogrom of the previous November.[21] The Germans welcomed the return of Henderson and showed it. And he, in turn, conveyed to London the firm indications of the peaceful intentions in high quarters, the pacific undertones in Hitler's speeches, and added his own assurances that there would be no hasty adventures by the Germans, though some day Memel and Danzig would have to return to the Reich. There appeared to be no undue preoccupation with the future of Czechoslovakia.[22]

[20] *History of The Times*, vol. IV, Pt II, pp. 551–60, see also *The Times* 9–13 March 1939.

[21] Feiling, p. 399.

[22] N. Henderson, *Failure of a Mission*, p. 200, and *Documents of British Foreign Policy*, (DBFP) vol. IV, pp. 110–11 and 120–1. Henderson reported that he had advised Ribbentrop and Goering to ignore the criticisms of 'the noisy opposition press' in London and the hostile attitude to Germany of Churchill and his friends; they 'carried no weight'.

How far these assumptions were from the realities can be measured by the progression of orders which were issued by the Reich Chancellery within a matter of weeks of the peace of Munich. The first of these was an 'Interim Directive' issued by Hitler on 21 October 1938. This ordered the armed forces and the economic ministries to be prepared henceforth 'at all times' to liquidate the Czechoslovak rump and to occupy Memel. They were also to be prepared for all eventualities arising from the defence of the frontier and protection against surprise air attack; but the central theme was Czechoslovakia. 'We must be ready at any time to crush the remnant of Czechoslovakia if her policy should become hostile to Germany ... The object is the swift occupation of Bohemia and Moravia.'

Four weeks later, on 24 November 1938, Hitler issued his 'first supplement' to the 'Directive' of 21 October. It was signed by Keitel: the Fuehrer ordered that apart from the contingencies mentioned in the original, 'preparations are also to be made for the surprise occupation of the free City of Danzig'. Three weeks later, Hitler added a further note to this directive. The preparations for the liquidation of Czechoslovakia were to be continued but 'on the assumption that no resistance worth mention is to be expected'.[23]

And then, on 13 March, on the day of *The Times*'s reassuring editorial, Ribbentrop sent a warning message to the German embassy in Prague, to be alert and to take care that no member of the embassy staff was available if the Czech government wanted to make any communication.

From Budapest, the Regent of Hungary, Admiral Horthy, cabled Hitler his 'sincere thanks' on that same day. The dispositions were made, he informed the Fuehrer. 'On Thursday, the 16th of the month, a frontier incident will take place which will be followed by the principal blow on Saturday.' And Horthy ended with more effusive thanks and assurances of his 'unshakeable gratitude and friendship'. And still that same day,

[23] The most convenient reference to these orders is still Peter de Mendelssohn's *Nuremberg Documents*.

Hitler spoke at length on the telephone with the Slovak Premier, Father Tiso, and urged him to declare Slovakia's independence and so precipitate the Czech crisis.

The rapid crescendo of the crisis was reflected that whole weekend in the press and radio of Germany, Poland and Czechoslovakia.[24] German troops, Slovak troops, Czech and Hungarian troops were on the move. A Slovak mission had arrived in Warsaw, another in Budapest; governments were dismissed and appointed. In the midst of the tumult, the League of Nations High Commissioner, the perceptive Swiss Professor Burckhardt, had arrived in Berlin. On the Sunday (12 March), he called on his old friend, the head of the German Foreign Ministry, Ernst von Weizsaecker, who told him that the final preparations for the occupation of Prague had been completed. They met again the following day when Weizsaecker discussed in considerable detail the possible consequences for Poland, Danzig and Memel of the planned occupation of Czechoslovakia. Burckhardt immediately reported these conversations to his superior in Geneva, the Political Director of the League Secretariat, Frank Walters.[25]

Two days later, Burckhardt was given a detailed account of Hitler's further intentions in Czechoslovakia, Danzig and Memel by the Nazi President of the Danzig Senate, Arthur Greiser. Burckhardt reported once more to Walters, who, in turn, advised the Foreign Office in London.

The extraordinary feature about the course of events that week was that there was so little effort by the Germans to keep them secret. A great deal of information about the troop movements, reports of the remarkably careless talk by important officials, and the evidence of the familiar rhythm of intervention must have reached the British and French Secret Services, the

---

[24] The Paris *Journal de Débats* had published on Thursday, 9 March, a detailed account of Hitler's aggressive intentions during March, and this received much attention in the Continental non-Nazi press. See for example *Neue Zürcher Zeitung* for 9 March and subsequent days.

[25] C. J. Burckhardt, *Meine Danziger Mission*, DTV Dokumente, p. 219.

Foreign Office and the Quai d'Orsay and the British and French embassies in Berlin and Prague – not to speak of the garrulous diplomatic world of Warsaw and Budapest. Yet, inexplicably, the British government was shocked and surprised – and so, of course, was Mussolini.[26] But the accepted view by some of our own foremost contemporary historians[27] that Hitler himself was taken by surprise by the sudden turn of events, and ordered the occupation of Czechoslovakia, so to speak, on the spur of the moment, is clearly not supported by the facts of the case. The evidence shows that the March crisis was premeditated and prepared. It had not been foreseen by Chamberlain and his friends. Its effect on the British Prime Minister was, however, not quite that which has been popularly accepted. There was still a curious after-play between Hitler and Chamberlain which greatly intrigued and puzzled Hitler to the end of his days.[28]

But first we must ask ourselves how it was that the great apparatus of information maintained by the Foreign Office and the Armed and Secret Services had failed to sound the alarm in either France or Britain. Churchill was bothered by this and raised the question in Parliament a month later, on 13 April. After twenty-five years' experience in peace and war, he said, his faith in the British Intelligence Service had remained unshaken. It was, he believed, 'the finest of its kind in the world'. Yet in the case of the subjugation of Bohemia 'Ministers of the Crown had apparently no inkling, or at any rate no conviction, of what was coming. I cannot believe that this was the fault of the British Secret Service', Churchill added, leaving his audience with the impression that he for one knew otherwise.

And speaking as he did immediately after the Easter weekend when Mussolini had invaded and occupied Albania, Churchill asked the question which has not been answered to this day.

[26] See Sir John Simon in the House of Commons.

[27] See A. Bullock, *Hitler, a study of tyranny* and A. J. P. Taylor, *The Origins of the Second World War*.

[28] *Hitler's Table Talk, 1941–1944* edited by Hugh Trevor-Roper, p. 254.

'How was it,' he continued, 'that on the eve of the Bohemian outrage Ministers were indulging in what was called "Sunshine talk" and predicting "the dawn of a Golden Age"? How was it that last week's holiday routine was observed at a time when clearly something of a quite exceptional character, the consequences of which could not be measured, was imminent?'

How was it indeed? But was Churchill correct in exempting the Secret Service from his censure? The curious feature on both occasions, however, was that not only did Ministers of the Crown remain in apparent ignorance of the critical events that were about to be unleashed, but so did the members of the Imperial General Staff and the Service Departments most intimately concerned. Neither the Army nor the Admiralty made any anticipatory dispositions in the case of Hitler's march into Prague or the Italian invasion of Albania a month later. On the contrary, the British Mediterranean Fleet was dispersed and one of its principal ships actually lay anchored in the port of Naples.

This was, however, not the end of the story; it was barely the beginning. We must assume with Churchill that the Secret Service was advised of Hitler's intentions and of Mussolini's plans. We know from Sir Alexander Cadogan that he received a 'hair-raising' warning from the Intelligence Service on Saturday, 11 March. We also know that the information was couched in terms that did not convince either Sir Alexander or his chief, the Foreign Secretary; and it made no dent on the Prime Minister's conviction that all was well. Or could it be that Chamberlain had expected this all along, and was prepared to accept it as the necessary final chapter of the Munich settlement? His first reaction does rather support this view. His subsequent indignation and change of front have to be seen as the outcome of two independent, unforeseen and unrelated occurrences.

The first was the spontaneous anger of the British public at Hitler's action; it spilled over into the Conservative Party, in Parliament and even into the Cabinet. Chamberlain had seen and remembered how these imponderable forces could destroy a political reputation after the Hoare-Laval agreement in 1935. He was not going to let any similar kind of groundswell develop; he would himself give the lead that would redirect it. And while he pondered on his next step, fresh information reached him from the Secret Service and through trusted private channels. These were to shape the next move.

Suddenly, Chamberlain was encompassed by alarms. The Rumanian Ambassador, V. Tilea, had come with information (which turned out to be false) that the Germans were about to present an economic ultimatum to his country. Reports from Danzig and Memel spoke of preparations for an imminent attack by the Germans. But far the most telling information reached him from his Secret Service – rather more pressing now after the earlier failure. Secret and semi-secret intelligence was presented to the Prime Minister to convince him that the occupation of Prague was but the prelude for an attack on Poland, possibly by the end of March. The German Army, Chamberlain was told, could mobilize in forty-eight hours; Poland might be attacked at any moment.

Chamberlain, Halifax, Cadogan and the Head of the Secret Service consulted on these reports which grew in volume and insistence as the month progressed.[29] Chamberlain could no longer afford to ignore them; but, now, he had also to take into consideration another aspect of the situation with which he had been confronted by the Americans.[30]

Chamberlain had recently received from the US Ambassador in London, Joseph P. Kennedy, an estimate prepared by the Intelligence Division of the American General Staff of the air strength of the Powers in Europe. It was an alarming document, similar in emphasis to that which Lindbergh had presented at the time of Munich. If anything, it was even more gloomy in its implications. Germany, according to this US intelligence estimate, had five times more bombers than Britain and eleven times more than the United States. German superiority in fighter

---

[29] Colvin, pp. 309–10.
[30] Elliot Janevay, *Struggle for Survival*, p. 24.

planes was similarly marked. Germany had indisputable mastery of the skies, the report said.

Chamberlain's own military advisers were not quite so extreme but hardly more encouraging. It was an admittedly difficult situation. Urgent action was necessary, but it involved risks which the Prime Minister felt were too great for the safety of the country. He had to make a stand, and he had to reassure Hitler at the same time. It was at this point that Chamberlain decided to work out a solution on his own. He stilled the popular clamour with a firm speech about Hitler's tearing up of the Munich settlement which he made on the eve of his seventieth birthday, on 17 March. But two days later he wrote a most revealing note to his sister.[31] He had come to understand that it was impossible to deal with Hitler after this latest experience, he told her. He had therefore worked out a plan which he had put to a few ministers that day, 19 March, and which he would put to the Cabinet on the following day. 'It is pretty bold and startling,' Chamberlain noted, 'but I feel that something of the kind is needed, and though I can't predict the reactions in Berlin, I have an idea that it won't bring us to an acute crisis, at any rate at once.' And then Chamberlain adds the significant afterthought that, as always, he wanted to gain time: 'I never accept the view that war is inevitable.'

He 'wanted to gain time'; but for what? He was by no means convinced that war was inevitable. It was not to fight that he required time; it was to prepare for a European settlement in which he, Chamberlain, would play the central role, not Hitler. The curious march to this end had begun. The Cabinet's Foreign Policy Committee with Chamberlain, Halifax, Hoare and Simon as the hard core, began consideration of Chamberlain's suggested guarantee to the Poles. There were doubts and differences of opinion on many points and, especially, about the participation of the Soviet Union.[32] The

---

[31] Feiling, p. 401.

[32] These have been fully and frankly recorded by Churchill, Feiling, Taylor, Maisky and others, and need not be repeated here.

implications were far-reaching; a fundamental departure from the practice of British foreign policy was at stake: whether to pass the ultimate decision on war or peace out of British control. Chamberlain was impatient with the doubters and the critics. According to a note sent by Lord Beaverbrook to Liddell Hart, the General Staff advised against a guarantee to the Poles because Britain did not have the resources to fulfil this commitment.[33] Hore-Belisha had asked for permission to circulate to the Cabinet the paper which gave expression to this considered opinion of the General Staff but Chamberlain had refused his consent because it would be tantamount to a criticism of his policy.

In the middle of this Cabinet debate, on 22 March, Hitler occupied the Memel territory. Some years later, Hitler recalled[34] that 'when I took possession of Memel, Chamberlain informed me through a third party that he understood very well that this step had to be taken, even though he could not approve of it publicly'. On 23 March, the day after Hitler marched into Memel, Mussolini received a personal letter from Chamberlain appealing for Mussolini's help in establishing mutual trust. The letter convinced Mussolini that the democracies had no will to fight and that therefore there was no risk in going ahead with the seizure of Albania on Good Friday, a month later.[35]

It is now on these seemingly contradictory actions by Chamberlain that we must focus. He was no Machiavelli. He was not blessed with undue subtlety in diplomacy. How, then, can we explain these opposing traits that marked his actions in the two weeks following the occupation of Prague which were to lead him to the Polish guarantee?

We must allow for all the human emotions which are usually cited to explain his actions at that time: anger with Hitler, concern over unfavourable public opinion, discontent in his own party, grave anxiety about possible further moves by Hitler,

[33] Basil Liddell Hart, *Memoirs*, vol. II, p. 221.
[34] Quoted in *Hitler's Table Talk*, p. 254.
[35] *Ciano Diaries, 1939–1943*, ed. Malcolm Muggeridge, p. 54.

and the wilful desire to reassert his own authority. Each played its part – often a powerful one – in reshaping Chamberlain's outlook. But none of them persuaded him to abandon his golden rule during the March discussions. He was still as concerned in preserving the peace now in March as he was then in September. He was as firmly convinced that 'given time' he could yet reach a negotiated settlement of the Polish crisis. His private letters show this. His instructions to his service advisers confirm it. His attitude in the Cabinet Committee of Foreign Policy demonstrates it; and some of his private expressions, reliably recorded, remove any lingering doubt.[36]

Wars – and especially the war of 1939 – are, more often than not, the product of imagined and misunderstood situations rather than of real ones. In 1939, the diplomatic and Secret Service identikit bore only superficial resemblance to the real culprit, but it was enough to frighten the British and the French into a combination of action and inaction. Thus, during these decisive weeks of March 1939, Chamberlain was made acutely aware of the Hitler intention to seize Poland. But the information was false. It referred to an imminent attack – 'any day now' – and it was to meet this immediate menace that Chamberlain decided to rush through his Polish guarantee.

It was this difference in the timing of the intelligence that reached him which led Chamberlain to make the greatest and most decisive error of the war – even though war had not yet come. It was the bitter irony of it all that the purpose of the Polish guarantee was initially to *deter* Hitler from attacking the Poles 'any day now' – in April – and to make him pause, preserve the peace and so provide the necessary time for a settlement of the Danzig and Polish questions.[37] The guarantee was not

[36] See Feiling; *The Ironside Diaries*, ed. R. Macleod and D. Kelly; and especially Richard J. Whalen, *The Founding Father*.

[37] Jones, pp. 431–2; Feiling, pp. 401–7; Templewood, pp. 328–9, and *Daily Express* and *The Times* for 31 March and 1 April. This appears to have been also the view of the Polish Premier, Colonel Beck, see L. B. Namier, *Diplomatic Prelude*, p. 244.

A report from the German Ambassador in Warsaw, von Moltke, sent on 30

conceived, as the record will show, to mobilize swift military help to the Poles should they be attacked, or to bring about Hitler's speedy defeat should he decide on war.

Since Hitler did not attack either Danzig or Poland at the end of March or early in April as the Secret Service and others had warned Chamberlain, he drew comfort from his action: the Polish guarantee had worked; it had deterred Hitler.[38] The planned attack had not taken place. Chamberlain's critics – and, more surprisingly, also his friends – have been inclined to overlook the powerful influence this development had on him in confirming the accuracy of his interpretation and the correctness of his policy. Months later, when the crisis had once more moved to the brink, in mid-July 1939, Chamberlain was still convinced that a solution was possible without war. 'If the dictators would have a modicum of patience,' he wrote to his sister, 'I can imagine a way could be found of meeting German claims while safeguarding Poland's independence.'[39] And a comment which Chamberlain made later, after war had broken out, to Joseph Kennedy, the American Ambassador, emphasized Chamberlain's persistence in the policy of gaining time for a negotiated settlement between Hitler and the Poles. According to Kennedy, neither the British nor the French would have made Poland a cause of war if it had not been for the constant needling from Washington. Chamberlain told Kennedy that 'the Americans and the world Jews had forced him into the war'.[40]

March, is particularly interesting in this context. He says that the British Ambassador, Sir Howard Kennard, had told him that day that the Poles would have to take account of the German character of Danzig, and it was necessary to prepare Polish public opinion for this – see *Documents of German Foreign Policy* (DGFP), vol. VI, p. 191.

[38] Though on 13 May Halifax had to cable Henderson in Berlin in order to impress on the Germans that the British guarantee also covered Danzig and that Britain was prepared to go to war, if need be. We shall see in the next chapter how this firm stand was backed up in reality. The Italians, incidentally, intercepted all Foreign Office cables and passed copies to the Germans – see DGFP, vol. VI, pp. 487–8.

[39] Feiling, p. 407.

[40] *Forrestal Diaries*, 27 December 1945, ed. Walter Millis, pp. 121–2.

B

Here again we come up against that curious ambivalence in Chamberlain. In his talks in the Cabinet and with the leaders of the Labour opposition,[41] he gave his colleagues to understand that, if Hitler attacked the Poles, they would hold out long enough for the British and French to mobilize their full strength and come to their aid. 'The Polish Government certainly understood the tactical limitations of any British intervention, but none the less welcomed our guarantee, and believed that it would deter Hitler rather than provoke him.' It was clearly understood, however, Sir Samuel Hoare claimed later, that the deterrent implied by the Polish guarantee was a world war against Germany, not immediate local aid for the Poles.[42] The Labour opposition leaders were told again, on 30 March, that the government had information that the German attack on Poland was imminent. And the following day, Chamberlain told Parliament of the terms of the guarantee to Poland. It was a curiously worded declaration.

Reuters news agency and *The Times*, both of which had particularly close links with the Prime Minister's office, produced 'interpretations' of the guarantee which could only have come from Downing Street. The British guarantee implied, these two reports suggested with an undertone of unmistakable authority, that the Poles would enter new negotiations with the Germans and show themselves rather more conciliatory. 'Only by offering concessions to the Germans could the Poles earn our guarantee.'[43] Concessions in Danzig and the Polish Corridor would not, in the British view, constitute a threat to Polish independence.

But Hitler had not waited for Chamberlain to make up his mind about the Poles. He had received a fairly accurate account of the heart-searching that was going on in the British Cabinet.[44]

[41] Hugh Dalton, *The Fateful Years*, vol. I, p. 237.

[42] Templewood, p. 350.

[43] Dalton, p. 239; see also Ulrich von Hassell, *The von Hassell Diaries, 1938–1944*, p. 42.

[44] E. Kordt: *Nicht aus den Akten* and DGFP, vol. VI, pp. 150, 172, 353.

On 25 March, while the British were still far from decided and preoccupied with reports of Hitler's plans for an immediate invasion of Poland, the Fuehrer called von Brauchitsch, his Supreme Commander of the Army. For the time being, Hitler told him, he did not want to solve the Polish question. But preparations for this should be started. 'A solution in the near future would have to be based on especially favourable conditions. In that case, Poland would be so completely knocked out that for the next decades there would be no longer need for her to be accounted as a political factor.'[45] He would *force* the Poles to accept his terms unless they were prepared to negotiate a settlement by midsummer. He added that preparations should be made accordingly, though he would have preferred not to use force in solving the Danzig problem for he did not want to drive the Poles into the arms of the British.

But neither Hitler nor his Supreme Commander had much faith in a peaceful solution. Nine days later, on 3 April, 'Case White' was ready in the form of a set of instructions to the Commanders of the Wehrmacht: they were to be prepared for operations against Poland 'not later than September 1'. Hitler, like Chamberlain, might have preferred a settlement based on a Polish acceptance of his terms without the need of having recourse to war. But, unlike Chamberlain, Hitler was certain that in the end he would have to use force – at least against the Poles.

Hitler, as can be seen from his timetable, did not wait for Chamberlain's Polish Guarantee before deciding on his plan of attack. For Hitler, unlike most of his contemporaries, thought in long-range concepts. The occupation of Austria, of the Sudetenland and of Prague were all steps to the final settlement with the Poles. They served other purposes as well, but as Jodl explained to the Nuremberg Tribunal, once the whole of Czechoslovakia had been taken, the strategic preconditions for

[45] Walter Warlimont, *Im Hauptquartier der Wehrmacht, 1939–1945*, pp. 34–5 (English ed. pp. 19–20); Robert J. O'Neill, *The German Army and the Nazi Party, 1933–1939*, p. 167.

an attack on Poland were complete. There remained only the political considerations.

That was the background against which the Anglo-French staff talks were about to commence, six months after the Munich settlement, and with a surprising absence of political guidance from their governments about their policy objectives. As a result, the two staffs remained riveted to three basic assumptions which they had accepted:

That the British were unprepared for war;

That the French were unable to fight a war;

And that the Germans had a vastly superior streamlined war-machine, in gear, ready to go and held back only by Hitler's disinclination for war.

2

The Legend of British and Anglo-French Unpreparedness

Unlike the politicians, the professional soldiers – including the sailors and airmen – were reputed to be the realists who reached hard-headed decisions, unswayed by emotion, guided only by a cool assessment of established facts. The Munich settlement, as we have seen, gave them time to catch their breath. They took it. The Imperial General Staff made the most of the interval thus gained at the expense of Czechoslovakia's military contribution.[1]

In February, four months after the sacrifice, the Chiefs of Staff presented the Cabinet with a comprehensive report on how they saw the post-Munich situation.[2] In this document, oddly described as 'European Appreciation', the three services placed the defence of Egypt and of the Suez Canal as first in strategic importance. India was fully considered, the prospect of sending naval reinforcements to the Far East was contemplated. The possibility of involvement in Europe was relegated to the conclusion that Anglo-French strategy should concern itself primarily 'with maintaining the integrity of French territory'; how this was to be done was expressed in impressive-sounding platitudes. There was no great sense of

---

[1] This, according to Hitler's speech to the Reichstag on 28 April 1939, comprised over 1,500 planes (500 of which were front-line types), 469 tanks, over 500 AA guns, more than 43,000 machine-guns, a million rifles, a thousand million rounds of rifle ammunition and more than three million rounds of field-gun ammunition.

[2] J. R. M. Butler, *History of the Second World War, Grand Strategy* (henceforth referred to as *Strategy*), p. 15.

urgency; it was as if Munich had given them all the time in the world. There was no feeling that the sands were running out; that Hitler's priority was not Egypt, but Prague; that Hitler's objective was not the Suez Canal, but Europe.

The point was eventually taken on 27 March: six months to the day after the Munich settlement, and two weeks after Hitler had torn up this agreement by his occupation of Czechoslovakia, the British and the French Staffs started 'discussions' to formulate joint plans to meet the new situation.[3]

Two days later, on 29 March, the Cabinet met in London and decided that in case of a continental war, British participation would no longer be restricted to the Navy and the Air Force. In future, the British would have to be prepared to dispatch an army to the Continent. The Cabinet also decided to double the strength of the Territorial Army and approved the Prime Minister's proposed 'guarantee' to the Polish State which was to be made public on 31 March.

Thus, in the Cabinet room at Downing Street, the British government opened its protective umbrella over the Poles, while across the road at the same time at the first meeting of the French and British Staffs, their 'military' advisers prepared to elaborate on the nature of the protection provided.

They began with a restrained exchange of information. The British Army's representative explained the smallness and slowness of the proposed British contribution, while the French disclosed, only 'in general terms', the strength of their forces in France. But they told the British nothing about their proposed plan of campaign. The British did not press them on this point – 'indeed, we felt we had not the right to do so'.[4]

[3] The talks were held at the War Office in London. The British delegation was made up of the Joint Planning Staff – Captain Dankwerts represented the Navy; Group Captain Slessor the Air Force; and General Kennedy the Army. The French delegation was headed by General Lelong, the French Military Attaché in London, and included Colonel Noiret and Colonel Aymé of Gamelin's staff. Others, including General Gamelin, participated from time to time. Lord Halifax requested all those taking part 'to wear plain clothes' so as to remain 'inconspicuous'; see DBFP, vol. IV, p. 228.

[4] Major-General Sir John Kennedy, *The Business of War*, p. 8.

The military reflections on the European situation appeared thus to be inspired by none of the anxieties that compelled Chamberlain and the government to take the dramatic step, one so much at variance with British foreign policy, of guaranteeing the independence of Poland. We have seen that the principal reason for the urgency of this declaration was the fear that an attack on Poland might be imminent. But having thus committed the British Empire to come to the aid of the Poles, neither Chamberlain nor the Chiefs of Staff in London and Paris appeared to have given a second thought to the manner of implementing the guarantee should this become necessary. By all accounts, we must conclude however that this was due not to Chamberlain's knavery or calculated double-dealing but to his conviction – that fatal feeling to which we have already referred – that the pronouncing of the British guarantee would suffice to deter Hitler from his proposed attack.

But the Anglo-French Chiefs of Staff cannot be excused on the same account.[5] Theirs was the responsibility to provide for the implementation of the guarantee – unless they had strict instructions from their governments that they were not to consider any such measure as might bring relief to the Poles while they were under attack from the Germans. And there is no record of such a governmental directive. One has the impression that there was no need for it: the British and French Staff delegations had written off the Polish guarantee as soon as it had been made. At no stage of their joint planning had they allowed it to affect their set opinions of the manner in which the French and British had to confront the seemingly overwhelming might of the German Reich and the Duce's Italy.

'We should be faced by enemies who would be more fully prepared than ourselves for war on a national scale,' they wrote at the end of their first joint meeting in their report to the two

---

[5] They had no reason to assume that the Poles could look after themselves for some weeks or months after the Germans attacked them, for they had realistic appraisals and urgent warnings of the vulnerability of the Polish defence from their own respective military attachés in Warsaw; but this advice was unheeded even if it was noted – of which there is no evidence.

governments. The Germans and Italians would have superiority in air and land forces but would be inferior at sea and in general economic strength. From this the two Staffs concluded that 'in these circumstances, we must be prepared to face a major offensive directed against France or Britain or against both.' And to defeat this German plan, they advised that Britain and France would have to concentrate all initial efforts during this time; 'our major strategy would be defensive'. They were prepared to make one exception, however, to this general rule: 'we should be ready to seize any opportunity of obtaining, without undue cost, successes against Italy which *might* reduce her will to fight.'[6]

But the course of the discussion between the two Staffs was if anything even more instructive of the contemporary outlook than were its summary conclusions. The British delegation informed the French[7] that the undertaking given a year before remained unchanged: Britain's initial contribution to a continental force could be no more than two regular divisions. In addition, under the new conditions of urgency, Britain would be ready to dispatch another two divisions in eleven months' time. On the other hand, the two armoured divisions which had been promised for 'as soon as possible' during the earlier exchange with the French government in 1938, would not be ready for another eighteen months, not before September 1940.

The French were understandably 'dismayed' by such an unpromising prospect – and the Poles were left in blissful ignorance. France's first objective in a war with Germany, her Staff delegation explained, would be the defence of French territory. 'When this had been secured they intended to remain on the defensive, though maintaining an economic blockade of Germany, till sufficient resources for an offensive had been built up.'[8]

[6] L. F. Ellis, *History of the Second World War: The War in France and Flanders, 1939–40*, p. 4.
[7] ibid., pp. 4–7.
[8] ibid., p. 4.

The Anglo-French Staff talks proceeded from these two starting positions. They had no difficulty in reaching agreement on the broad strategic policy which the Allies should follow and in their appreciation of the probable German action, both of which were incorporated in the summary conclusions which were submitted to the two governments.[9]

It would be idle to claim that the French had not been shocked by what they learned about British preparedness at these London talks. Like the British public, they had been impressed by the formidable programme and claims made by the Service Ministers and the press during the discussions of the Service Estimates in Parliament earlier that month. These had created the impression of a massive and determined forward move in the rearmament programme – nineteen divisions for an expeditionary force, vast new air fleets to dominate the skies, £250,000 a day spent on the new navy.[10] During the initial stages of the Staff talks the French remarked on the contrast between this confident public presentation and the gloomy paper on British potential which confronted them.

The British delegation, therefore, endeavoured to assuage the French dismay about the smallness of the British effort on land by stressing the extent of Britain's potential at sea and in the air. 'Great Britain was now making a greater effort in the expansion of the Royal Air Force than she had ever made before . . . She was on the way to obtaining a bomber force comparable to Germany's,' the French were told. But this new instrument was to be used with only the greatest reserve. The British and French Staffs agreed that the Allies 'would not initiate air action against any but purely "military" objectives in the narrowest sense of the word, i.e., naval, army and air force establishments'. Attacks would be restricted to those 'which would not involve loss of civilian life'.[11]

[9] ibid., p. 4.
[10] See particularly the reports – and headlines – on the Commons debates on the Service Estimates during the early part of March.
[11] *Strategy*, p. 17.

While the British and French Staff experts concluded their first deliberations on this considerate note, their opposite numbers in the Wehrmacht were putting the finishing touches to 'Case White'. It was ready for Hitler's signature on 3 April. Hitler, as we have seen, had decided on the broad lines of his course of action by 25 March 1939, when he outlined his views to Brauchitsch before asking him to prepare a more specific directive. He wanted to keep the British and French dangling, he wanted them misled and paralysed by confidential and contradictory information about Germany's intentions, *he* – not Chamberlain – wanted to make the most of the time and the benefits he had obtained at Munich.

Accordingly, he set the timetable for Brauchitsch: nothing rash at the moment so as to give the British, French and Poles every opportunity to make further concessions. For he was not yet ready for the solution of the Polish problem. But the time had to come to start preparations to this end which should be based, as we have seen, on the execution 'under especially favourable conditions'. Poland was to be 'crushed so completely that she would be eliminated as a political factor for decades to come'. The question of the deportation of the Polish population and the resettlement of the country were questions that Hitler wanted to be left open. It was with these guiding lines in mind that the Wehrmacht Staff set to work at the same time as the French and British Staffs met to consider the same problem – though one might not have thought so from the tenor of the London discussions.

Thus, at about the same time as the Anglo-French Staff delegations submitted their report to their governments,[12] General Keitel, the German Chief of the Wehrmacht Staff, completed his 'Directive for the Armed Forces, 1939–40'. It is instructive to compare this with the assumptions which were

[12] This is all the more noteworthy since the official historian, J. R. M. Butler has drawn attention (*Strategy*, p. 11) to the faithful manner in which, in the event, in September, the British and French followed the pattern set at that meeting – unshaken by the very different course the Germans had taken from that which the Anglo-French staff talks had anticipated.

simultaneously made by the British and French Staffs with regard to the German plan of attack.[13] So as to leave no doubt about the serious intentions underlying *his* exercise, Hitler added a codicil in which he indicated the timetable which he envisaged for the operation. The first part of the long directive restated Hitler's guiding lines to Brauchitsch of 25 March; it then proceeded to its military conclusions and to the stipulated tasks of the armed forces; a separate section dealt with the proposed occupation of Danzig which might become possible, independent of 'Case White', through the exploitation of a favourable political situation.

But Hitler wanted to be sure that his instructions were not misunderstood; this was not a hypothetical Staff exercise,[14] one of the many war games with which army staffs like to amuse themselves and confuse the historians. This was the real thing; hence the codicil with its timetable. There were three specific instructions which the Fuehrer had added, Keitel noted at the end of his 'Directive': preparations were to be made in such a way 'that the operation can be carried out at any time from 1 September 1939, onwards'. To this end, the High Command of the Wehrmacht was to draw up 'a precise timetable' for the attack on Poland and synchronize the operation of the three branches of the Wehrmacht. All these plans, and all detailed timetables, were to be ready for submission to the Supreme Command of the Wehrmacht by 1 May 1939. Hitler was not playing games. He had given the Wehrmacht four weeks to prepare its blueprints and he had set a date for the operation. In his assumptions, Hitler was much nearer the mark than were the Anglo-French Staffs. Why?

[13] See *Strategy*, p. 4; also Ellis, pp. 4–7.

[14] A. J. P. Taylor has argued with regard to the Hossbach memorandum that this was no more than a hypothetical plan in which all military staffs indulge in their efforts to anticipate every possible development – and there may be an element of justification in this. But it cannot be argued in the planned attack on Poland, initiated with 'Case White'. This was not hypothetical and Hitler's timetable provides decisive confirmation of its single-minded purpose: to destroy Poland not later than September 1939.

One rather extraordinary answer suggests itself at this stage. Hitler forbade at this time any kind of military intelligence against the British; and he appears to have largely ignored the mountain of reports which Himmler's *Sicherheitsdienst*, (the SD), and Ribbentrop's Foreign Ministry were collecting in the United Kingdom. If there had been not one single report from all these sources, Hitler would have been no worse off with regard to his knowledge about the thinking and planning in London. Yet Hitler, judging from his actions, was clearly in the picture about British intentions, British capacity to sustain them and the government's unwillingness to do just that during those decisive months.

It would be straining our credulity too much to attribute Hitler's perceptiveness entirely to his political and military intuition – of which he undoubtedly had more than his fair share. We must assume therefore that he had other, more accurate sources of information than the 'usual channels' which he treated with unmitigated contempt. The question arises whether he had not his own 'Canaris' or 'Gisevius', or possibly someone even more favourably placed in the British governing circle, who kept him advised about British affairs? It is – in the light of Hitler's reactions – an irresistible conclusion. Nothing else could account for Hitler's certainty and self-assurance in assessing the actions of the Chamberlain government. For the moment, it is a thought that will have to remain with us.

It was different in Paris. Here the Germans had a first class intelligence apparatus that kept them fully informed with regard to the French government and the situation in the armed forces. They learned a good deal from these sources about British plans and intentions, for anything that the British passed on to the French soon reached the German intelligence organizations.

This was, however, only one side of this preparatory battle for position. The British and the French, fortunately, had some able and shrewd young service attachés in Berlin, who did not share the rather more relaxed approach to German policy of some of their seniors at the Berlin embassies or in their home departments. The British military attaché was Kenneth Strong (who was later to become the Director of Military Intelligence until his retirement in 1966), and the French had as a member of their air attaché's office Paul Stehlin, who was later to become the Chief of Staff of the French Air Force, and who was in Berlin on special mission for the *Deuxième Bureau*.[15] He accompanied Daladier to Munich and he had exceptional connections with the Germans and with his own government.

It was Stehlin who, later, realized that throughout the Munich crisis and for almost a year that followed, the Germans had reversed the process of intelligence. Far from keeping military secrets from the British and the French, they made every attempt to publicize them and to convince the Allies of the reality of Germany's military capacity and, especially, of her air power. Instead of hiding information from the Allied attachés, the Germans supplied them with confidential information which they wanted the governments in London and Paris to receive from their own unsuspected sources. We have seen how Goering's aide, Bodenschatz, intervened to impress the German view on Stehlin, and the impact which this had on the French. But, now, with the Anglo-French Staff talks under way, with preliminary soundings in Moscow for the inclusion of the Soviet Union in the ring to contain German expansion, German 'frankness' took a surprising new turn.[16]

It followed an earlier talk which Bodenschatz had with Stehlin at the end of January 1939, during the quiet period between the Munich settlement, and the occupation of Prague. General Bodenschatz advised Stehlin that a radical reorganization of the Luftwaffe was under way. It was intended to treble Germany's air power by 1941, though they had all the means 'to do it tomorrow', should this be necessary. Bodenschatz then asked that what he had told Stehlin should be transmitted as verbatim as possible to the government in Paris. Germany wanted an understanding with France. Germany had great

15 See Stehlin.
16 ibid., pp. 160–2.

sympathy for the French. The visit of the commander of the French Air Force, General Vuillemin, to the Luftwaffe had created a far better impression than that of the Italian officers who had preceded him.

The Fuehrer, Bodenschatz continued, had the greatest confidence in 'President Daladier'; he considered the personality of the head of a foreign government to be a decisive factor in the military evaluation of a country. Bodenschatz added that Hitler would not have followed the same policy of intimidation towards Britain if the man at the helm had been 'a Lloyd George and not a Chamberlain'. Germany had need of peace for her internal development. Hitler must have peace to carry through his gigantic architectural plans that would be compared in generations to come with the age of Pericles and Louis XIV.

Bodenschatz added that Goering remained the natural and accepted successor. Goering had been the first to denounce the November pogrom against the Jews and he was endeavouring to get rid of Goebbels from the governing circle. Bodenschatz assured Stehlin that he was full of optimism about the future.

Stehlin transmitted the information as requested by Bodenschatz. Whatever Stehlin's personal reservations might have been, the French Ambassador in Berlin, Coulondre, the government in Paris, and the ally in London, accepted the Bodenschatz assurances at their face value.

Six weeks later, immediately after the Germans had occupied Prague, Bodenschatz approached Stehlin once more with an entirely different set of confidences. One would have thought that these would be received with greater reserve in view of past experience – but there was no evidence of this. On the contrary, the information which he now gave to Stehlin 'full of joy and in a talkative mood' soon percolated to the second round of the Anglo-French Staff talks in London and played its part in the shaping of the Anglo-French assessment of the developing situation.[17]

The Bodenschatz theme had switched its emphasis from

[17] Stehlin, p. 161–2; *Strategy*, p. 17.

'peace' to 'defence'. The Germans, he told Stehlin, would remain strictly defensive in the west. 'The West Wall was nearly complete' and any attack on it could be parried with relatively weak forces. This would leave the Germans with 150 divisions which could break through any blockade in the east. Against the Western Powers, the Germans would strike with the air force, a 'blitz' – Bodenschatz used the word – attack on England would be decisive. For this purpose *'Luftflotte Nord'* was being equipped with the most modern aircraft, the Junker 88.[18]

Just over a month later, on 30 April, Bodenschatz intervened again with Stehlin, with the most surprising confidences he had yet volunteered to the French Secret Service. They were, in a way, an elaboration of the earlier theme. Hitler was now convinced that the alliance of Britain and Poland would lead them into armed conflict with Germany, Bodenschatz told Stehlin; but Hitler had said all along that he would go to war 'only after he had all the trumps in his possession'. He was determined to remove any risk of a prolonged war on two fronts. Therefore, there were only two options left open: either the British and French persuaded the Poles to make the concessions which Germany demanded, or Germany must reach an understanding with the Soviet Union. 'Talks to this end are already under way,' Bodenschatz explained; 'one day you will hear that things are happening in the east.' There had been three partitions of Poland; there was no reason why there should not be a fourth, he added by way of a concluding pointer.

Stehlin reported this to the French Ambassador in Berlin. Coulondre was deeply impressed and sent Stehlin with the report and the Ambassador's personal comments to the Foreign Minister in Paris. Stehlin waited for six days to be received by Bonnet but without avail.[19] Frustrated, he returned to Berlin. But far more important for our purpose is to see what happened to his report of the talk with Bodenschatz, and, most particularly, to establish the purpose for the intervention by

[18] Stehlin, pp. 181–2.
[19] Stehlin, p. 186.

Bodenschatz. What did he, or Goering, or Hitler hope to achieve by the calculated leak of negotiations with the Russians that had not even started in earnest? What did they seek to gain by this risky anticipation?

For the answer we have to turn away from the world of make-believe in which the military, possibly even more than the civilians, lived in that April 1939. The reality was Hitler's continuing preparations for the attack on Poland on 1 September; the reality was the cumbersome, painful evolutions of the Anglo-French Staff talks; the reality was the pace of rearmament and the deployment of forces in Europe. We need to look at these more closely before we can return to the curious case of the information which Bodenschatz gave to Stehlin on Hitler's reorientation towards the Soviet Union. For the Bodenschatz 'leak', as we shall see, was intended to set in motion a chain of events designed to paralyse any Anglo-French intention to take effective measures in support of the Poles by giving Paris and London advance notice of a projected agreement with the Soviet Union, which in fact, at that time was little more than an intention in Hitler's mind. But it was a remarkable *tour de force* in military diplomacy. It served its purpose. It increased French and British – especially Chamberlain's – mistrust of the Soviet Union. It also signalled the Russians, in a manner that involved no commitment for the Germans, of what Hitler had in mind, for they soon heard in Paris of the Bodenschatz-Stehlin conversation.

By this time Hitler had taken the measure of his opponents in Paris and London. He proceeded now to set them up, to bait them and tempt them – and scare them. He made use of 'confidential' information that was filtered through to London and Paris; he gave assurances and he had warnings transmitted through unsuspected neutral channels; and, for good measure, he made his own public declarations – especially in the remarkable defence of his foreign policy in the Reichstag on 28 April.

At the same time, he had all but made up his mind that the favourable moment for attack on Poland was approaching. On

11 April, he issued his own personal instructions about the completion of 'Case White'; more details for the attack on Poland were added to the original; and still more at the beginning of May. And across the channel, where the Anglo-French Planning Staff met again in April and continued its discussions into May, the Allies either walked or fell into every trap that Hitler had set for them. They did what he wanted them to do; they read the situation as he wished them to read it. It was not altogether fortuitous. The British were no fools, nor were the French. They were hard-headed realists, not romantics. They could not afford the anti-Nazis' wishful thinking. Yet they were misled into the gravest of all errors by the apparent authenticity of the information that was transmitted to them. Once again, that ubiquitous apparatus of diplomatic dispatches, intelligence reports and well-informed private sources, combined to provide the impressionist picture which the Germans had wanted the British and French to accept as genuine – and they did.

It was without question this presentation of the situation, in all its facets, that made possible Hitler's swift victory in 1939 and again in 1940. It was in March and April that Hitler succeeded in neutralizing the Western Allies and thus prevented their *active* intervention in September when it might have proved fatal to his further plans – and possibly also to his régime.

Let us see then how the information fed into the secret channels in Berlin came out at the other end in London, at the continuing Anglo-French Staff talks.

By the end of April, the British had materially upgraded their promised contribution though the time-lag was still considerable. An attempt was made at these meetings to strike a preliminary trial-balance of the Allied and German deployments as they stood at that moment. The Anglo-French experts concluded that the French would have seventy-two divisions facing the Germans and the British would provide another four divisions, making a total of seventy-six divisions; another twelve French divisions would be stationed on the Italian

frontier. Against this, the Anglo-French Staffs estimated that
the Germans would be able to mobilize at least 116 divisions.
If the assumption of overwhelming German superiority was not
unduly stressed, it was there for all to see.[20]

The impression of German superiority was further emphasized by the presentation of the estimated balance of strength in
the air. Front line units available to the Allies and the Germans
were reported to be:

	German	Allied
FIGHTERS	1,000	856
BOMBERS	1,900	824
ARMY COOPERATION AND RECONNAISSANCE	800	954
TOTAL	3,700	2,634

The Joint Staffs did not think that the Germans would attack
France 'until Poland was disposed of', but once this had been
done, Hitler would be able to attack the Allies with something
like a hundred divisions. The Joint Staffs could not foresee how
soon Hitler would feel free to launch his attack but they left
their respective governments 'with the sobering knowledge' that
when the time came, the Germans would have the double
advantage of initiative and superior strength.

There was, however, no suggestion that the temporary
German preoccupation with Poland should be exploited; there
was no extensive assessment of how great this German diver-
sion would be; there was no serious consideration of the possibility that Germany's 'superiority' would be – temporarily but
decisively – affected during her war against Poland. This
omission emerges even more strongly from the discussions
concerning the role of the Anglo-French air forces at the Joint
Staff meeting in March, and at the subsequent discussions in
April and May.

[20] *Strategy*, pp. 10–11.

The RAF Bomber Command had earlier prepared some rather perceptive if optimistic plans on how it could destroy the nineteen power plants and twenty-six coking plants of the Ruhr by flying three thousand sorties in a fortnight.[21] But now that it came to the crunch, an entirely new factor intervened. The combination of Bodenschatz and Lindbergh began to tell. The Air Staff had produced estimates of German available air power that were to have a wholly intimidating and paralysing effect on the French and British governments – just as Hitler had intended. The Air Staff's calculations showed that the Germans could maintain a daily attack on London with a thousand bombers daily for fourteen days[22] – a terrifying picture in the spring of 1939. It was this planted exaggeration of the Luftwaffe's capacity that henceforth controlled most of the Allied thinking and planning. It was this that led to the decision which so delayed the dispatch of the British Expeditionary Force to France and sent them by the long round-about route through the western Atlantic ports in order to avoid possible air attack; it dissuaded the French from letting the RAF use French airfields for planned attacks on German targets, and it led to the progressive – if one may use this word in this context – elimination of Bomber Command from playing any purposeful role at all during the decisive preliminary phases of the war.

Having built up a strategic bomber force, the two Staffs agreed that its main purpose was to contribute to the success of the land battle. The bombers were to wait until the French were attacked and then bomb German points of concentration, communications and airfields. But these were thought to be not very profitable targets by the British Air Staff, and the French were told, in effect, 'that they must not expect much result from the assistance of British bombers'.[23]

The Bodenschatz-Lindbergh shadow began to hang ever

---

[21] Sir C. Webster and N. Frankland, *The Strategic Air Offensive against Germany*, vol. I, p. 97 – this is what Hitler feared most – see p. 57.
[22] *Strategy*, p. 17.
[23] *Strategic Air Offensive*, p. 104.

more threateningly over these talks. The question arose most acutely after the British had guaranteed Poland's independence. The Joint Air Staffs considered the new commitment and rightly concluded that it might lead the Germans to launch their attack in the first instance against the Poles. In that case, however, the British General Staff advised that 'nothing could be done to assist Poland'.[24] The French delegation spoke of their plans of making some proving attacks on the Siegfried Line but it was clear to the British that these would not seriously threaten the Germans or greatly, if at all, relieve the pressure on the Poles; and the British delegation stressed that intervention by the British Army could not make any appreciable difference to the German onslaught on the Poles.

That still left open the question of Britain's principal contribution to Allied power – helping Poland by a strategic bomber offensive. But both the British and French Air Staffs were firmly against a policy that would require the use of French airfields to make it effective. The Committee of Imperial Defence was unhappy at this blunt refusal to engage the British and French air forces in support of Poland and the report was referred back to the Joint Planning Staff for further consideration.

At the same time, however, instructions from the two governments laid down that no bomber operations should be undertaken which would involve German civilian casualties and so invite German air attacks on British cities and ports. In the opinion of the British and French governments their countries were far more vulnerable than was Germany. Bomber Command was therefore ordered to turn its attention to engaging the German Fleet. That was thought to be safe; it would not lead to retaliation against London or Paris. It also, of course, ruled out any kind of assistance that mattered to the Poles. Goering, Bodenschatz and Lindbergh had done their work well. The RAF had been paralysed; Bomber Command would not move during the critical opening days of the war when Germany would be at its mercy.

[24] Chief of Staff Memo. 3 June 1939, see *Strategic Air Offensive*, p. 105.

The Poles were told none of this, but the rather embarrassed evasions and assurances from British and French quarters began to disturb them. All the more so, since their intelligence reports indicated rather more specific German preparations for an attack on Poland; this was particularly noticeable in Slovakia where the German preparations had reached dimensions that were difficult to hide – and which the Germans appeared to make no great effort to screen. The Polish leaders were in a curiously divided state of mind: they appeared still convinced that the Anglo-French guarantee would deter Hitler from attacking Poland and that his rather too open preparations for such an attack were designed to intimidate them rather than annihilate them; that, in short, Hitler was engaged on a gigantic bluff in order to force the Poles and their guarantors to make concessions in Danzig and the Corridor.

But the Polish leaders had also a nagging doubt that they might be wrong; wrong about Hitler and wrong about their new allies in the west. They could do little to discover what was in Hitler's mind, but they could seek clarification from the French and the British. Accordingly, the Polish War Minister, M. Kasprzyski, virtually invited himself to Paris, and arrived there on 14 May for talks with the French military leaders.

The French were rather embarrassed by the direct confrontation with the Poles, for they had just concluded a series of special discussions with the British Staffs and had reached agreed conclusions about their joint inaction should the Germans direct their attack first against Poland – which the British thought to be the more likely German intention; the French were less sure about that. They evidently feared a sudden German descent on France.

But the upshot of these Anglo-French discussions before the arrival of the Polish War Minister in Paris was that 'there could be no question of hurried attack on the Siegfried Line'.[25] This was precisely the issue which the Polish War Minister was coming to discuss. In the event, however, General Gamelin and

[25] *Strategy*, p. 11.

the French Air Force Commander were rather less than frank with the Poles. General Vuillemin assured them – within a matter of weeks of the London discussions when the opposite had been agreed – that the French Air Force would from the outset act vigorously to relieve any pressure on the Poles. Gamelin himself engaged in a good deal of double talk which provided him later with an alibi but which left Poland's War Minister under the clear impression that the bulk of the French Army – some thirty-five to thirty-eight divisions – would launch a second front against the Germans not later than sixteen days after their attack on Poland.[26]

The Polish mission returned to Warsaw, still a little uneasy about the lack of enthusiasm in Paris – and especially about the failure to obtain a clear political commitment, but they were content with the military assurances which they thought they had received from General Gamelin and the French Air Force commander, General Vuillemin.[27]

The Poles had, in fact, gone much further in their assumptions as to what would happen at the outbreak of the war than Gamelin was later prepared to admit, either at the Riom Trial or in his memoirs. They appeared to have a much clearer – and more accurate – scenario of the German alignment on the outbreak of hostilities. They put these to the French during the Paris discussions, and they put them before the British a few days later, at the end of May, when a British delegation representing the three Services came to Warsaw for further talks on the implementation of the British guarantee.

The Poles anticipated a German attack against them with some seventy-seven divisions. Against this force, the Poles claimed that they could mobilize fifty-two divisions, though they were short of heavy artillery and tanks. But their principal weakness was the lack of adequate stores in reserve. They had enough to keep forty divisions in the field for only three months.

[26] Namier, *Diplomatic Prelude*, pp. 459–62.

[27] General M. C. Gamelin, *Servir*, vol. II, pp. 424–6; Georges Bonnet, *Quai d'Orsay*, pp. 236–8.

Without adequate Allied help, the British mission concluded, the Poles would be out of the war at the end of six months – or sooner.

But the central point of the Polish argument was that with so many German divisions concentrated against Poland, there would be only around twenty-five to twenty-eight divisions available to the Germans on the western front and this presented an exceptional opportunity to the French Army and the British Air Force, both of which would enjoy a temporary superiority of three to one on land and in the air. The British delegation thought that there would be rather more Germans left for the defence of the Siegfried Line, between thirty and thirty-five divisions, but they did not impress on the Poles the conclusions which they had reached in their earlier staff conversations with the French: that it was doubtful whether the Allied Armies in the west 'would or could do much more than contain the lowest number of German divisions required to man the Siegfried Line.'[28]

Summer was drawing near – the dangerous weeks for Europe when the country soil becomes suitably firm for swift movement by invading armies. Yet the prospect of war continued to be discussed by governments and military staffs with an air of unreal matter-of-factness which, on the Anglo-French and Polish side, added up to an inherent disbelief that war would actually break out. Without saying so in as many words, the military discussions and the political and diplomatic exchanges were dominated by the continuing belief in the deterrent effectiveness of the British guarantee to Poland. So deeply had this confidence bitten into the British diplomatic pattern that, as we have seen,[29] the Foreign Secretary, Lord Halifax, found it necessary to stress the British determination to go to war if the independence of Poland was threatened, or if Poland was attacked. But the Germans, who saw the British instruction the day it was sent, thanks to the unexpected efficiency of the

[28] *Strategy*, pp. 55–6
[29] ibid.

Italian Secret Service, took this warning in their stride. For we are approaching the fateful date when Hitler made it clear to his armed forces that he was no longer deterred by the British threat. He had assessed it and he was not frightened any more.

The May discussions, therefore, proceeded on curiously distinct levels. We have followed the course of the military talks between the British, French and Poles, and those between the British and French without the Poles. The two sets of talks came to very different conclusions: the Poles were left with the feeling that, however reluctantly, the British and French would come to their aid, if they were attacked by the Germans. They were also somewhat reassured because they believed that under such conditions the Germans would not launch an invasion of Poland.

The British and French, in the absence of the Poles, reached a rather different conclusion. They were agreed that they could do nothing for the Poles while they were under attack other than ensure the defeat of Germany in the long run. But they were not too much bothered by this conclusion because they also believed that there would be a political settlement on the lines desired by Chamberlain and by the French government. The Joint Staff talks, which had started late in March and gone on through April and May, had, as a result, the air of a rather academic exercise in which few of the participants really believed. The French proposals made by Gamelin and Vuillemin in the discussions with the Polish War Minister, struck a similar note.

But for the moment, the decisive element in the equation was the Polish confidence that the Poles had British and French backing and that there would be no war over Danzig. This complacency in Warsaw was further encouraged by the visit of the Soviet Deputy-Commissar for Foreign Affairs, Vladimir Potemkin, to Warsaw on 10 May, just before the departure of the War Minister for his talks with General Gamelin in Paris. Potemkin's talk with Poland's Prime Minister, Colonel Beck, was unusually cordial and greatly reassured the Poles. He expressed the Soviet Union's full understanding for Poland's difficult position and favoured the continuance of their relations which he considered good, correct and normal.

Beck was particularly pleased that the Soviet Minister assured him that the Soviet government had full understanding for the position which the Poles had adopted towards the proposed Russian alliance with Britain, France and Poland after Beck had explained to Potemkin that the policy of the Polish government was not to enter into any special relationship with either of her two powerful neighbours, neither with Russia nor Germany. Potemkin, moreover, advised Beck, on 'instructions from his Government', that in case Poland were the victim of an armed attack, the Soviet Union would adopt a policy of benevolent consideration towards Poland.[30] It was a discussion that cast curious light on Soviet intentions at the time and especially on the Soviet protests about the unreasoning attitude of the Poles during the British negotiations for joint action with the Soviet Union.

But other events were meanwhile shaping Poland's fate. While the Polish War Minister was negotiating and planning a somewhat imprecise and inconclusive collaboration with France, the German and Italian Foreign Ministers, Ribbentrop and Ciano, had met in Milan on 6 May and agreed on a detailed Treaty of Alliance which was signed in Berlin on 22 May. But rather more significant was the turn which the preliminary discussions had taken over the conclusion of a German economic agreement with the Soviet Union. On 20 May, the Commissar for Foreign Affairs, the newly appointed Molotoy,[31] suggested to the German Ambassador that before they could complete an economic agreement they would have to create the necessary political basis for it. Molotov refused to elaborate further, but the German saw its significance and took the hint. Ten days later, on 30 May, the State Secretary at the Foreign Ministry in

[30] Polish White Book, Doc. 165.
[31] He had replaced the Jew, Maxim Litvinoff, in an abrupt change, on 6 May the day Ciano and Ribbentrop met in Milan.

Berlin cabled the ambassador in Moscow: 'we have decided to put out feelers to the Soviet Union . . .'[32]

What Bodenschatz had told Stehlin in April as fact was beginning to happen now; but neither in London nor in Paris was there any real awareness of the turn of events. On the contrary, there was a shift of opinion in quite a different direction. The British ambassador in Warsaw was making efforts to bring about a new compromise based on a joint Polish–German declaration.[33] His German colleague in Warsaw reported a new mood of hopefulness about the prospects for a *rapprochement* to Germany. The Poles were making advances through the good offices of the Italian and Japanese governments; in Paris Pierre Etienne Flandin, a former Prime Minister, expressed his confidence in the peaceful intentions of Hitler and Mussolini.

In London, however, Chamberlain spoke firmly in winding up a foreign affairs debate in Parliament on 19 May. He warned Germany of the possible consequences of her policy and that armed conflict would be disastrous to all concerned. But then came that curious tailpiece which showed again which way Chamberlain's mind was turning. 'I do ask the House to remember,' he pleaded, 'that in this matter we are trying to build up, not an alliance between ourselves and other countries, but a peace front against aggression, and we should not be succeeding in that policy if, by ensuring the cooperation of one country, we rendered another country uneasy and unwilling to collaborate with us.' And he returned again to his theme of 'a peace front' that would avert an outbreak of war, 'not an alliance'.

What Chamberlain meant could be best understood from the Anglo-French Staff talks. Clearly in military terms they made no sense as a 'peace front'; the only way they could be understood in Chamberlain's terms was a means of bringing the Poles to the negotiating table with the Germans. And under these conditions war would be averted only by

[32] DGFP, vol. VI, p. 608.
[33] ibid., pp. 568, 569.

massive and self-denying concessions by the Polish government

Thus, in the middle weeks of May, the governments believed one thing, and led others to believe them, while the reality was shaping events in quite different directions. Once again, we search in vain through the dispatches of the diplomats and the reports of the intelligence services for any clue of what was really taking place, what Germany was planning to do, what the Allies had to guard against, what the Russians were contemplating. Neither in London nor in Paris did the governments show any apparent awareness of what lay in store for them. But in Berlin, where Hitler had again paid no attention to the reports of his diplomats and spies, the German Fuehrer prepared an appreciation that showed understanding for, or very detailed inside information about, the mind of the British and French governments – and of their military advisers.

Hitler had summoned his military leaders for 23 May. Most, though not all, of the principal military personalities were present in his study at the New Reich Chancellery, but no civilians, not even Ribbentrop. Goering, Raeder, Milch, Brauchitsch, Keitel, Halder, Bodenschatz, Jeschonnek and Warlimont, were there; Schmundt took minutes.

The purpose of the gathering, Hitler told them, was among other things, to review the present situation and to set the tasks for the armed forces arising from it. Hitler appeared to have made up his mind about Poland and about Britain. The Pole was the enemy; he had always been Germany's enemy. Treaties of friendship had not changed this. They had to be clear that it was not Danzig as such that was at issue; it was Germany's need for living space in the east; 'if fate forces us into a showdown with the West it is good to possess a largish area in the East.'

The question of Poland could not be dissociated from the showdown with the West. There was therefore 'no question of sparing Poland'. Germany was left with the decision 'to attack Poland at the first suitable opportunity'. Germany could not expect a repetition of the Czech crisis: 'there will be fighting. Our task is to isolate Poland.'

Hitler then elaborated and stressed the keynote to his thesis, as he described it. 'It must not come to a simultaneous show-down with the West (France and Britain).' The conflict with Poland, Hitler insisted, 'beginning with an attack on Poland, *will be successful only if the West keeps out of the ring*'.[34] It was this that they had to bring about. It was going to be 'a matter of skilful politics'.[35] What Hitler was telling his soldiers was, in effect, that military and political considerations could not be separated, and that in the given circumstances they must understand that political measures had to take precedence; that his political steps would set the scene for decisive action by the armed forces. Hitler proceeded to do this, though not with complete frankness towards his soldiers. We know more now of the circumstances which prevailed at the time than they did, and Hitler's speech to them on that 23 May makes more sense to us in view of what we know than it did to his military leaders who were still in the dark about some of the main elements of Hitlerian diplomacy.

Thus, in a curious passage Hitler tells them that economic relations with Russia are possible only if and when political relations between them are improved. He was hopeful about this and he did not rule out that 'Russia might disinterest herself in the destruction of Poland'.

The interesting feature of this was that Hitler had formulated the problem in exactly the same words which Molotov had used to the German Ambassador on 10 May,[36] and that he was no longer thinking in hypothetical terms about 'the destruction of Poland'. Insofar as the British guarantee affected his thinking at all, it was directed against Britain, not against Poland. And even here, he made up his mind to a point where the act of going to war was left open only as regards its timing; he had

[34] My italics – J. K.; the same argument was used again by Hitler in 1941 when he planned his attack on the Soviet Union – and he came very close to success because of Western hesitation over the opening of a 'second front'.

[35] DGFP, vol. VI, pp. 574–80; see also E. M. Robertson, *Hitler's Pre-War Policy*, p. 173, for comment on the official translation.

[36] DGFP, vol. VI, pp. 574–7.

already decided to occupy Belgium and Holland, either by agreement or by force.

After 23 May, there was in fact no room left for a peaceful settlement in Europe except by the surrender to Hitler's demands on Danzig and Poland – and whatever might follow from such an Anglo-French capitulation.

But there were still fifteen weeks left for the exercise of 'skilful politics', to persuade the British and French – and also the Russians – of the correctness of their own legend that they were unprepared for war, and encourage them to stand aside – for whatever reason – while the Germans proceeded with the destruction of Poland. The manner in which this Hitler-inspired autosuggestion was received in the west can be seen best in the case of Britain's Foreign Secretary, Lord Halifax. He knew nothing of Hitler's speech to his officers on 23 May; but Hitler's 'Pact of Steel' with Mussolini, the day before, had convinced Halifax 'that war was coming', and that spring and summer would be a period of waiting.

Halifax proceeded to await its outbreak, we are told, with calmness and almost a sense of relief that the dice had fallen. He later prepared a memorandum in which he reviewed this period. In it he had argued that neither the Polish nor the Rumanian governments had been under any illusion as to the measure of concrete help they might expect from Great Britain in the event of Hitler choosing war. For the Poles, the British guarantee was the best chance, 'indeed the only chance', of warning Hitler off the decision to make war.[37]

It was not only Halifax who appeared singularly unaware of the logic of his own argumentation. Britain gave her guarantee to the Poles, he reasoned, in order to deter Hitler from attacking Poland. But now at the end of May, Halifax had reached the conclusion that the guarantee had failed in its purpose; Hitler was set on attacking the Poles; what now? Could the British and French do nothing but wait with calmness and a sense of relief, as Halifax's biographer puts it, for Hitler to strike? There

[37] *Halifax*, p. 437.

was nothing else because the politicians and soldiers in London and Paris had created the legend of Anglo-French 'unpreparedness'. They were, at heart, afraid of the unknown. They had a false and monstrously unreal picture of German might and preparedness, and even more so of German intentions and air power. More surprising was their lack of faith in their own capacity and in their own people – and allies – and their own incapacity or unwillingness to grapple with the situation that faced them. One is left with the impression of Allied governments, military leaders and secret services bamboozled and groping fearfully, like blind men, walking straight into Hitler's welcoming arms. He had little occasion to make use of skilful politics; Allied blindness and incompetence and self-induced fear served him better.[38]

And so, at the end of May, the legends had taken firm root: the British were believed to be unprepared, the French weak and of no matter in the power equation. The Germans were rated to be strong, prepared and determined and Europe's fate was laid at Hitler's disposal. It is time we turned from legends to realities.

[38] Only a short time before, Lt General Waldemar Erfurth had published his important treatise on *Surprise in War* in which he argued and demonstrated that it was important to induce the enemy to make decisive mistakes before a crushing victory could be won.

3

The Legend of German Preparedness

By the end of May, Hitler and Germany's armed forces were
prepared for war, but not for the kind of war the British or
French expected and not the kind of war with which the Anglo-
French Staff discussions were concerned. 'Case White', the
planned destruction of Poland, had been revised, amended,
polished and made ready for application – but only under the
most severely limiting political and economic conditions. For,
as the plans were developed with ever more detail, as the
military needs for 'the Blitz-like operation' were more precisely
stated, the German leadership became increasingly aware of the
gravity of the risk they incurred, and the narrowness of the
margins within which they were about to operate.

Two sets of facts had emerged with a starkness that could
not be evaded: the German economy was in no state to sustain
a long war, and the German armed forces were in no condition
to fight a simultaneous war on two fronts: against Poland in
the east and against the French and British in the west. Moreover, Hitler, at this time, was careful not to believe his own
propaganda. If anything he made the same mistake as his
opponents. A remarkably detailed estimate of French and
British strength had been prepared for him[1] which, though
strikingly accurate in most ways, greatly exaggerated the
strength of the RAF – or at least its preparedness to strike
offensively against Germany – and the size of the French

[1] Ulrich Liss: *Westfront 1939–40*, p. 25–6.

armoured forces. Hitler had already accepted the claims made by British and French Ministers as to their quickening pace of rearmament, and he compared them with the gloomy accounts presented by his economic advisers about the state of Germany's war economy.[2]

Basic raw materials were in acutely short supply. Steel was desperately short and new production would not be available for at least two or three years.[3] The oil position was critical. A report prepared for Hitler by the Wehrmacht estimated Germany's war requirements at twenty-three million tons annually; of this ten million tons had to be aviation gasoline. As against that, they could be sure of only three million tons, less than half the normal peace-time requirements for the country. Reserve stocks would cover no more than three to five months' requirements. Similarly, iron ore, magnesium and rubber were adequate for only a very short time – a few months at the most.

Hitler was also worried and apprehensive about the manner in which the British and French might strike at Germany if they were able to adjust the course of war to the pace of their own development. For months before and immediately after the outbreak of the war,[4] Hitler was preoccupied with the thought that Germany might be swiftly defeated by a series of air and land attacks directed at the Ruhr.[5] Hitler recalled these thoughts in a later 'Directive'. The moment the Ruhr came within range of heavy French artillery, or persistent British air attacks, it would cease to be 'an active factor in the German war economy', and there would be no means of replacing it.

About the same time – in November 1939 – Hitler again addressed his commanders and reviewed the period leading to

[2] See F. Klein, *Germany's Economic Preparations for War*, pp. 174–5; A. S. Milward, *German Economy at War*, pp. 7–8, 16.

[3] *The Effects of Strategic Bombing on the German War Economy*, prepared by the United States Strategic Bombing Survey, p. 69 et seq. See also Klein, Milward.

[4] United States Government Printing Office, *Nazi Conspiracy of Aggression*, vol. VII, p. 805.

[5] As we have seen (ch. 2, p. 43) this had been one of the Bomber Command plans which the RAF was forced to jettison.

the outbreak of hostilities, but he dwelt with special emphasis on the one point which had so worried him in this summer of 1939, while he was still uncertain about the British and French reaction.

'We have an Achilles' heel,' he told his generals, 'the Ruhr. The progress of the war depends on the Ruhr. If England and France push through Belgium and Holland into the Ruhr, we shall be in the greatest of dangers ... If the French army marches into Belgium in order to attack us, it will be too late for us.'[6] Especially in the light of such fears, the reports of the state of the Westwall, the Siegfried Line, were anything but reassuring. It had been completed at only a few key positions, particularly in the Saar. But these sectors were little more than window displays for the whole line. The rest was still, as General Jodl had described it, 'little better than a large building site'.[7] It was the intention to complete the first line of defence by the autumn: that was as much as he had been promised.

In order to round off the picture as it was presented to Hitler in the summer of 1939, we must consider the assessment of the French Army which his experts had prepared for him. After a searching and detailed analysis of every facet of French armed strength, the German Intelligence estimate concluded that, taken as a whole, 'the French Army must be rated the same as in the first world war, as the most formidable of all our potential enemies', and able to mobilize close on a hundred divisions within a matter of two weeks.

This was the reality of German preparedness, of Hitler's irresistible strength, of the terror of the Luftwaffe, which had made so fatal an impact on the governments and the military Staffs in London and Paris. But what mattered most during these first weeks of June was that despite all his directives and preparations, Hitler was still uneasy and uncertain. He was more than ever convinced that at all costs he must avoid a *simultaneous*

[6] This speech was made in November 1939, see *Nazi Conspiracy*, vol. III, p. 578.

[7] *Trial of Major War Criminals*, vol. XV, p. 361.

C

war on two fronts, or a long *defensive* war. The qualifications in both cases were of decisive significance.

But none of this state of doubt percolated through to the men who were influencing the shaping of policies in the Allied capitals. They, on the contrary, were impressed by the views of men such as Adam von Trott who, during the first days of June, visited his friends the Astors at their country home at Cliveden. There are two significant accounts of these discussions. Tom Jones wrote a short memorandum on 6 June 1939.[8]

'Adam von Trott,' he noted 'a young officer of the German Army General Staff who is over here to collect political impressions for the General Staff (not the Government) suggests to me privately that the situation is as follows . . .' Jones then enumerated the views presented by Adam von Trott. Hitler had decided to act that summer and neither the General Staff nor the public could alter the course of events in the coming weeks. Hitler's strategy, von Trott explained, was to overrun the wheat-growing, coal-mining and oil districts of Eastern Europe and the Balkans; if necessary, the Germans would defeat the Russians inside six months and occupy the Ukraine. After that, Germany could hold out in a war of any duration.

The only way this could still be averted, von Trott told Jones, was by impressing upon the Fuehrer personally the reality of Allied strength and thus demonstrating to him the risks which he was running by embarking on war. He suggested that this could be done by telling Goering that the Germans had the wrong idea of British strength and showing some leading Luftwaffe officers the capacity of the RAF (without divulging secrets). That might have an impact on Hitler; and so might a coalition government which would include representatives of 'our "warmongers" and of the Left'. Trott himself was impressed by the united and determined stand of the British, 'but the contrary was believed by the Leader and his entourage'.

Adam von Trott arrived in London on 1 June, called David

[8] Jones, p. 436.

Astor with whom he had been at Oxford, and spent the weekend at Cliveden. A number of Cabinet ministers were among his fellow guests there, including Lord Halifax, the Foreign Secretary, Lord Lothian, who was about to be appointed as Ambassador to the United States and Sir Thomas Inskip, the former Minister of Defence and now Dominion Secretary. Apart from the general conversation at the table, Trott was able to talk privately with Halifax and Lothian, and later also with the Prime Minister, Neville Chamberlain.

Trott returned to Berlin on 9 June and three days later presented a long memorandum of his conversations in England, together with a shortened version and a summary of his conclusions. The last two were submitted to Hitler, and we must assume that they were therefore written with the object of influencing him. What matters, therefore, in this context is not the accuracy or the political inclination of these reports and conclusions, but the impression which they conveyed to Hitler in Berlin, and the impact which Trott made on the English statesmen in London.

Unfortunately, it seems, Trott had the wrong ideas of Hitler's intentions. We have no means of knowing whether this was due to his own unawareness of the changed outlook as reflected by Hitler's briefing on 23 May, or whether he was an unsuspecting instrument in providing his British friends with wrong information deliberately planted by Walter von Hewel, Ribbentrop's personal liaison officer with Hitler, who had proposed the journey to London, rather on the lines of the information which Bodenschatz had fed to Stehlin and others. But the unforeseen outcome of Trott's journey was to reassure his friends in London rather than alarm them; his reports on the encounters in England must have had the same effect on the Fuehrer.

Trott's private discussions with the Prime Minister and the Foreign Secretary evidently made no great impact on them; he confirmed them in their views that Hitler would turn east and be heavily engaged there for some time, and so provide extra time for the British and French to reach their full state of preparedness. The suggestion that either of the two Luftwaffe commanders, Milch or Udet, should be invited by the RAF and shown what it could do, must have sounded odd to the fearful men at the helm who felt themselves greatly outnumbered by the Luftwaffe.

Similarly, Hitler must have felt that perhaps things were not quite so bad as he had feared, if Chamberlain and Lothian were still thinking of a settlement on the basis of greater independence for the Czechs and Slovaks. Hitler was already preoccupied with his proposed settlement of the Polish question, and assurances by British politicians that they conceded Germany a free hand 'economically' must have been welcome to Hitler as a step in the right direction – as was Trott's quotation from Chamberlain that Eden, Churchill and Duff Cooper were of no account and could be completely ignored. Trott found that 'the Fuehrer's clear-sighted refusal of any half-hearted understanding with Britain has now, in view of the threatened total conflict, brought about a genuine revival of the desire for a total understanding as the only alternative to war'. Against the gloomy realities of the German situation which Hitler had been reviewing, Trott's conclusion must have come as a ray of sunshine, just the opposite to what Trott had intended.

And, judging by a letter which Lothian wrote to Smuts immediately after his talks with von Trott, his attempts to impress the British had also sadly misfired. Instead of producing a firm front, a realistic appreciation in Britain of the nature of the Blitz-like war that the Germans were preparing, von Trott left Lothian with impressions that led him to say this in his letter to Smuts: 'The next crisis of "nerves" may come at any time – probably on the Polish question. My own view is that directly Hitler intervenes by force we should deter the Poles [*sic!*] from war and put down a blockade ourselves, making it perfectly clear that it will be lifted directly Hitler removes his troops and is willing to discuss a settlement by pacific means.'[9] That would not necessarily lead to war, in Lothian's view,

---

[9] J. R. M. Butler, *Lord Lothian*, p. 233.

because there would be no bloodshed. Provided there was a firm front of Britain, the Dominions and the Americans he personally believed, he told Smuts, 'that Hitler will withdraw and refrain from precipitating a world war'. And that, of course, would be the end of Hitler, Lothian concludes.

But in the privacy of his letter, Lothian, who was an intelligent man, conceived the possibility that Hitler might, after all, go on to destroy the Poles while standing on the defensive in the Siegfried Line and attack London and Paris from the air; what then should the Allies do, he asked? His answer was that they should first smash Italy. Once they had done that, Russia would join the Allies and 'Fascist Imperialism will wither away', which would enable Britain to make a lasting settlement with Germany.

This, then, was the impact that the Cliveden weekend and the private talk with von Trott had left on Lothian and his circle, which, according to Trott's report, included the Prime Minister. It evidently contributed little to the understanding of Hitler's intentions, or to the realization of the extent to which the fate of Europe was precariously balanced on the actions of the Allies to counter Hitler's set intention to destroy Poland. But neither von Trott nor his British hosts appeared to be aware of the nature of the crisis that confronted them: it was Hitler's crisis more than theirs. Hitler wanted to know the answer to one question which mattered more than all others: not whether the British would declare war if he attacked Poland, but whether the French and British would take immediate military action in the west while he was fully engaged in the east.

The answers that von Trott, and also other visitors to London during these weeks,[10] had brought back had greatly eased his mind. All the more so since none of them really knew which answer Hitler wanted to hear. Hitler evidently did not worry unduly about the reports of British determination not to give way this time, or about the popular mood to fight rather than appease again. All that he had already anticipated in the address to his officers on 23 May. It was the other side in which Hitler

[10] DGFP, vol. VI pp. 674–85, but particularly 682–5.

was now intensely interested and it was a much less well known but far more perceptive German observer in London who, later that same month, on 29 June, provided Hitler with just the information for which he had been waiting.

Hitler had, admittedly, taken the intellectual plunge into war at that May conference with his senior officers. But he was aware of their uneasiness and conscious of his own nagging doubts. Then just about four weeks after Trott's report came that of Hans Seligo,[11] the virtually unknown press director of the British section of the *Auslandsorganisation*.[12]

Seligo went straight for the heart of the matter. 'Preparations,' he began, 'are now being made in Britain in every field as if war were imminent.' The people were ready for a break at any moment. But there was an exception, Seligo pointed out at once. The popular feeling was not yet reflected 'in the determination of the Government to go to war at once'. Far from it, in Seligo's opinion. 'It can be said with a fair amount of certainty that Chamberlain himself, and the inner decision-making group of the Cabinet, are definitely working to prevent the outbreak of war, and would prefer a compromise over Danzig and the Corridor acceptable to their people, to any recourse to force.'

Seligo then proceeded to compare some of the reports which were being sent to Berlin from the German embassy with the realities of the situation as he saw it. 'Germany's official diplomatic representation' was convinced that negotiations with the British could be continued indefinitely and that the British government was inclined to reach an understanding with Germany on the future maintenance of peace. But Seligo warned against taking this assessment at its face value. He recalled that most Germans arriving in Britain 'to gather information' were astonished and deeply impressed by the British fighting spirit 'which they met everywhere'. And he proceeds to enumerate the basis of the new British strength.

Seligo, judging by his reports, was a quiet, factual reporter

---

[11] DGFP, vol. VI, pp. 874–8.
[12] The organization of the Nazi Party abroad.

who did not feel the need to soften, embroider and flatter to please the recipient. There is a convincing baldness in the facts which he proceeded to present to his superiors in Berlin. British preparedness, he reported, had reached 'a certain maximum' which, given the overall situation, he considered to be not unimpressive. Apart from the standing army, there were 275,000 recruits ready for training; the air defences were manned round the clock, coastal observation stations and air raid protection organizations were mobilized. Britain's air defence could ward off attacks for a long time, though not prevent them altogether. The Navy could effectively blockade Germany and keep its own Atlantic supply lines open while holding German submarines at bay. The Maginot Line was adequate to prevent any advance by German troops into France and leave sufficient French and British troops free to man the vulnerable zones in the north and south.

But one sentence buried in Seligo's report was undoubtedly all that mattered to Hitler at that moment; it rounded off Seligo's earlier reference to Chamberlain's preference for an alternative to war. By themselves, Chamberlain's inclinations were not enough evidence for Hitler to act upon; after all, he might change them from one day to the next. But here was something else, something that could not be changed before the deadline of 1 September. Seligo, in his dry way, reported that 'great gaps in armament remain, especially in the army in the field, but that is not so very important (to the British) because their tactical plans, particularly at the beginning of the war, do not assign any sizeable tasks to the British army in the field.'

It may have appeared to Seligo as 'not important'; it was a vital piece of information for the Fuehrer. French and British sources began to tally. Both had effective military instruments available for use against Germany: the French on land and the British at sea and in the air. But all that mattered now to Hitler was the matching confirmation from London and Paris that neither Chamberlain nor Daladier were going to use them for a war on two fronts while the balance of power was tilted against the Germans by the commitment in Poland.

There is no telling which of the reports – and there were a good many in similar strain at this time – decided Hitler. But they all pointed in the same direction – that if he struck against Poland, there would be no intervention from the west – although the military possibility for this was always there. That was a risk – a great risk. Soon after the return of von Trott, Hitler ordered two parallel sets of action. He gave orders for the intensification of the *rapprochement* with the Soviet Union to ensure his freedom from intervention from the east, and he made important changes in his plans for the attack on Poland to avoid a last-minute intervention by the West.

These were detailed in a further elaboration of 'Case White' which Keitel had prepared for the senior commanders of the armed forces. This gave the preliminary timetable of the attack, though it did not give the actual time for the start of the assault on Poland. But the significance of this document dated 22 June 1939, lay in the added 'suggestions' of the Fuehrer. He had changed his tactic. He was no longer intent on intimidating the British and French by an open demonstration of his intention as before Munich. He wanted to reassure them to the last possible moment, until it was too late for them to change their minds and come to the aid of the Poles by forcing the Germans to a war on two fronts, or worse, by falling on to Germany's largely undefended rear while she could not disengage in Poland. This was his nightmare. It was necessary, therefore, to avoid everything which might prematurely alarm the Allies.[13]

Hitler gave orders that nothing should be done to alarm the German population; the call-up of reserves was to be carefully camouflaged from employers and civilians generally; they were to be told that this was solely for the purpose of the autumn manoeuvres. He also ordered that 'for reasons of security the clearing of hospitals in the frontier area which the Army High Command proposes to carry out from the middle of July, must

[13] Stehlin, pp. 198–9, noticed this difference in mid-July.

be postponed.' It would be certain to disquiet the population and reach the ears of the Allied Intelligence.[14]

These had been the days of decision for Hitler. He had set course for a Blitz attack on Poland; he had set the lines for isolating her militarily from her western allies and politically from possible aid by the Soviet Union. But he also reached the conclusion that in the longer run war with Britain was unavoidable. Poland, he explained to his soldiers at the 23 May briefing, would be the first stepping-stone towards a greater struggle with the British; that would require a revolution in the organization of the German economy and armament programme.

Accordingly, the day after Keitel had issued his timetable for the Polish war, on 23 June, the Reich Defence Council met in special session. Goering presided and most of the civilian and military leaders were in attendance.[15] Goering told them that war was imminent and that it would require total mobilization of the country's resources. It was their job to deal with it. Seven million men were to be called up, and the shortcomings in the war plants and in agriculture were to be corrected by the transfer of labour from Czechoslovakia and the concentration camps. But all that the conference really succeeded in doing was to highlight the inefficiencies and shortcomings of the German war economy and of its armament programme. The measures on which it decided would not have any immediate effect other than dislocating the economy during its transition to total economic mobilization.

All these were added reasons for Hitler to persist with his overall concept of the *Blitzkrieg*. Its full implication has been best described in a recent study by Alan S. Milward,[16] in his analysis of the German economy at that time. It was mistaken, he argues, to assume that the Blitz was a simple military tactic designed to deliver a quick knock-out blow from a position of strength. The *Blitzkrieg* was a strategic as well as a tactical

[14] Keitel, '*Directive*' on '*Case White*', 22 June 1939.
[15] *Nazi Conspiracy*, vol. VI, pp. 718–31.
[16] Milward, pp. 7, 16.

instrument. It would enable the Germans to make the most of their greater preparedness for a short war, 'starting with surprise and ending with a quick victory'; it was a method of avoiding total economic mobilization.

But above all else, the concept of the 'Lightning War' was to prevent strong combinations of powerful forces opposing Germany *at the same time*. It meant that a successful attack could be carried out with comparatively small forces, providing the planning was sufficiently flexible to adjust the *Blitz* to the needs of each separate opponent.

It was effective against a weak, unsuspecting, cowed and unwilling enemy. It worked against Austria and against Czechoslovakia. It was expected to work against Poland. Hitler had hoped that it would work psychologically also against France and Britain; and in a limited sense it did so. It kept them out of the Polish war, but not out of the war. It was this adjustment which Hitler had made when he had ordered Goering to summon the Reich Defence Council for its June meeting. They were to be hastily summoned again a month later when the full extent of the unpreparedness of the Westwall had become apparent.

By mid-summer, then, Hitler had decided to go ahead with the attack on Poland despite the shortcomings in the German economy, the unpreparedness of Germany's western defences, and the inability of his armed forces to fight a war on two fronts. Hitler knew the risks he was taking, the hostages he was giving to Chamberlain and Daladier; but did they know of the opportunity that was within their grasp? We shall have to see.

After the rather negative conclusions of their paper of 4 May, the Anglo-French Staffs met again in June to consider the situation in the light of the intervening events, especially the discussions with the Polish War Minister in Paris and the talks of the British and French missions in Warsaw. The agenda for this midsummer meeting reflected no inkling of suspicion of the decisions which Hitler had taken in May, or that detailed preparations for the attack on Poland were well under way.

If intelligence to this effect had reached London – and one must assume that it did – then it was either misrouted, ignored, lost or unappreciated. It played no part in the consultations of the French and British Staffs at the June session.

They were still preoccupied with the implications of the Polish alliance. They cautiously conceded that it might have a certain advantage for the Western Powers. If the Germans launched their initial attack against Poland, 'as the British Chiefs of Staff thought most likely', it would give the French and British more time to complete their preparation and might seriously weaken Germany's striking power. But they were sure that Poland would be eventually overrun unless Germany was forced to fight also in the west and compelled to relax her pressure on the Poles.[17]

There seemed to be little hope for anything of the kind. Gamelin, speaking for the French, maintained that their main attack would have to be aimed at the Italians; an assault on the heavily fortified Siegfried Line would take long preparations and could not be undertaken in haste; the most the French could promise on the German front were some limited probing offensives that were unlikely to disturb the rhythm of the German attack in the east. This conclusion was further reinforced by the confirmation of the earlier decision of the Joint Air Staffs to confine allied air attacks 'to military objectives in the narrowest sense'.[18] The meeting ended with three propositions which were placed before the French and British governments:

1 The fate of Poland will depend upon the ultimate outcome of the war, and that this, in turn, will depend upon our ability to bring about the ultimate defeat of Germany, and not on our ability to relieve pressure on Poland at the outset.

2 The longer Italy remained neutral, even if her neutrality showed benevolence toward Germany, the better it would be for the Allies.

[17] *Strategy*, pp. 11–12.
[18] ibid., p. 12.

3 This meant the abandonment of the only counter-offensive measures on the part of the Allies contemplated by them in the early stages of the war, apart from economic pressure.

The staffs also considered the alternative hypothesis that the Germans might first attack France. They considered it unlikely but, should it occur, then the Germans would have to retain some thirty to thirty-five divisions in the east and that again would be a beneficial by-product of the Polish guarantee. But the upshot of this further round of talks was again negative in terms of immediate action, or even plans for action. The recommendation that the Allies must win the war was, one would have assumed, hardly necessary; but in the context of the Polish guarantee, it sealed the fate of Poland.

If this guarantee received such cavalier treatment at the hands of the Anglo-French Staffs, it was appraised far more seriously in Berlin. It evidently worried the Germans. Hitler himself recast his whole thinking about the future in the light of the British undertaking. He was forced, as we have seen, to switch German military and economic thinking from an exclusively Blitz strategy to one of combined Blitz and long-term planning, a combination that proved, in the event, to be insurmountable.

But Hitler still believed that firmness on his part would make the British and French buckle; that even if they stood by their undertaking to Poland, they would not fulfil it in a way that would interfere with his plans; and the changed circumstances would provide for him new opportunities to avoid a long war. Hitler's policy of thus seeking to undermine the British guarantee was most effectively and, apparently, unwittingly supported by Hitler's German opponents.

We have seen the impact which the von Trott mission had made on his British friends; and the impression his report must have conveyed to Hitler. Trott, we know, came at the instance of members of the opposition and the General Staff – and with the approval of the chief of Ribbentrop's personal cabinet, von

Hewel. Within a week of von Trott's return, on 15 June, and after his report had been circulated in Berlin, another private German emissary left for London. Dr Erich Kordt was a senior official of the German Foreign Ministry, and his brother held an important position at the German embassy in London. He came to see Sir Robert Vansittart, who represented the opposite political spectrum from that which von Trott had encountered at Cliveden; but the ultimate targets were the same – Halifax and Chamberlain. He came at the suggestion of von Weizsaecker, the shrewd, underrated, head of the German Foreign Office, who was such a master at dissimulation that he has to this day foxed all possible investigations into his actual outlook and purpose. Although he does not mention Kordt by name, von Weizsaecker becomes almost passionate in his otherwise colourless memoirs when he comes to describe the evident purpose of the mission.[19] 'I had to make clear to the English that they had given a blank cheque to the Poles by their promise of aid. They had thus placed the authority for the unloosening of the war in the hands of irresponsible foreigners.' The British had to be told to keep the Poles on a close rein. He wanted to warn off the Poles without encouraging Hitler, and to convince Hitler that the British were not bluffing. One gets the impression that von Weizsaecker was better informed about the outlook of the British cabinet than of that of the Fuehrer.

This then was Kordt's principal mission, but not the only one. He was also charged to warn the British that the Germans were negotiating with the Russians and preparing a deal. This was hardly news, but was still no more than one of a number of similar reports that were reaching the Foreign Office. In fact, the very frequency with which these reports appeared on the diplomatic rumour front, beginning with Bodenschatz's antici-patory confidential warning to Stehlin, tended to discount the credibility of reports. The British Ambassador in Paris had reported indications of a German–Russian arrangement on 7 June; the British Ambassador in Berlin noted in his dispatch of

[19] Von Weizsaecker, *Erinnerungen*, pp. 236–7.

13 June that he felt that 'the Germans are getting at Stalin'. And then on 16 June, Kordt was telling Vansittart that he had his information 'from the horse's mouth'.[20]

In a statement made on oath after the war, Halifax confirmed that he had received the message Kordt had given to Vansittart.[21] But in view of the general state of affairs – and especially of Russian assurances that they wanted to reach an agreement with France and Britain – it was the other part of Kordt's message, the warning about the Polish guarantee, that received far more attention. He had impressed on his British friends that the Polish guarantee had failed to deter Hitler, that Hitler saw it as a provocation. This, in the opinion of Kordt's influential German friends, might lead him to precipitate action. It was necessary, therefore, Kordt explained, in the opinion of his friends on the General Staff, in the Foreign Ministry and among the leaders of the opposition, to avoid anything which might provoke Hitler and lead to war. What Kordt did not spell out was any kind of convincing alternative of what Hitler would do, if the British held back on their guarantee and restrained the Poles. We know now what Hitler was planning: did von Weizsaecker, did Kordt? Did they really believe that Hitler's 'Case White' depended on Polish 'provocations'? One can sympathize with the scepticism and distaste with which Vansittart treated the Kordt mission.

But it had disastrous consequences. For Kordt, coming in the wake of von Trott, appears to have still further strengthened British and French military hesitation to back up the guarantee. One consequence could be seen in the discussions with the Polish Technical and Financial Mission which arrived in London only a few hours before Erich Kordt. The Poles wanted to make arrangements for urgent supplies of material and for substantial credits. But there was no sense of immediacy in the British response. The aircraft that it was eventually agreed to

[20] Kordt, *Nicht aus den Akten*, pp. 312–19.
[21] For further details see also Wheeler Bennett, *Nemesis of Power*, p. 444; and Colvin, pp. 324–5.

supply never reached Poland in time; credits were severely restricted. The Poles asked for £50 million initially; they settled for £8 million. The question of immediate military assistance for the Poles, should they be attacked, was not discussed at all, though the Polish delegation pressed hard for some clarification.[22]

The Chiefs of Staff decided, moreover, to make this position absolutely clear to the Committee of Imperial Defence. They told the Committee early in July that the fate of Poland must depend on the ultimate outcome of the war, and that this would depend on the Allies' ability to defeat Germany in the long run, not to relieve pressure on Poland at the outset.[23] Moreover, the Chiefs of Staff felt that something might be done to help the Poles indirectly by means of air attacks on Germany. But this, they said, raised the whole question of bombing policy; and they proceeded to consider the alternatives from restricted and limited air attacks on the German Fleet and other indisputably military targets down to a policy of 'taking the gloves off' from the outset and to strike at the German war effort where it would hurt it most even at the cost of heavy German civilian casualties.

The Chiefs of Staff, however, rejected all courses which might have brought effective relief to the Poles because by so doing they would invite dangerous German retaliation on the Allied cities and industries, and, moreover, risk the alienation of neutral opinion.[24] At no point in the memorandum of the Chiefs of Staff was there any discussion of the possible advantages to the Allies of compelling Hitler to fight simultaneously on two fronts, or questioning the more alarmist sources on which the decision to opt for a long war at the price of jettisoning Poland was taken.

The Committee of Imperial Defence approved the report 'as a basis for discussion with the French and the Poles'[25] whom –

---

22 See *Strategy*, pp. 55–6; and Namier, *Diplomatic Prelude*, pp. 246–7.
23 *Strategy*, p. 56.
24 ibid., pp. 56–7.
25 ibid., p. 57.

in the words of the official historian – 'it was thought important to deter from any "impetuous action" which might give the Germans an excuse for indiscriminate retaliation'.[26] The French, when advised of the findings of the Chiefs of Staff Committee, gave their relieved approval together with an assurance that they would confine themselves to only the most limited operations on land and in the air. 'It was agreed that . . . as an immediate step Poland should be informed of the restrictions accepted by the French.'[27]

The Polish government was however neither consulted nor told in precise language that there would be no military relief for them from the West should they be attacked first. Instead, it was decided to send General Sir Edmund Ironside, who was soon to become Chief of the Imperial General Staff, to Warsaw to talk to the Polish military to find out what they had in mind. Ironside was not instructed to inform the Poles of the report by the British Chiefs of Staff and of its endorsement by the French.[28]

He went to Downing Street on 10 July, six days after it had been decided to send him to Warsaw, for a briefing by the Prime Minister and the Foreign Secretary.[29] Chamberlain told him that the government had no idea 'what the Poles were going to do' and he wanted Ironside to find out. He also explained his own contorted attitude to Hitler. Undertakings by Hitler were of no use; there would have to be a practical guarantee that if Danzig returned to Germany, the Poles would have the same rights as they have now. 'It should not be beyond the brains of the Allies to devise some guarantee that would bind Hitler', Ironside noted Chamberlain as saying.[30] But then Chamberlain felt sure that Hitler had an acute political sense and did not want war, and yet, a few moments later Chamberlain spoke of war being almost inevitable. About Russia, however, he had no

26 The language, it will be noted, was that of Trott and Kordt.
27 *Strategy*, p. 57.
28 *Ironside Diaries*, 4 July 1939, p. 76
29 ibid., p. 77.
30 ibid., p. 77.

doubts: the one thing Britain could not do was to come to an understanding with the Soviet Union.[31]

The following day, Ironside reviewed the papers dealing with the latest Anglo-French military exchanges and found to his satisfaction that there would be no hasty offensive against the Siegfried Line and that other forms of assistance, such as air attacks, would take a long time coming.[32] 'I must get the Poles to realize that haste is against them,' Ironside noted in his diary on 13 July;[33] on the seventeenth he flew off to Warsaw – to find out what the Poles were planning to do, or tell them what the Allies were not planning to do. On Tuesday, 18 July, Ironside had his first meeting with Marshal Smigly-Rydz, the Polish Commander-in-Chief.

After his meeting, Ironside cabled the government in London that he was certain that the Poles would do nothing rash in the military sense, that their military effort was little short of prodigious, that Britain should not make so many restrictive conditions to the financial aid to the Poles and that 'time is short'. And he added that the Poles were strong enough to resist if attacked.[34]

But Ironside was a worried man in Warsaw. He found that neither the French nor the British had told the Poles the harsh truth of their proposed desertion. The French had lied to the Poles[35] and assured them that they would start a counter-offensive against Germany if Poland were attacked. He was hardly less disturbed when he came back to London on 24 July and saw the War Secretary, Hore-Belisha, who was about to attend a meeting of the Committee of Imperial Defence at which the Polish question was to be discussed. Ironside was shocked by the 'amazing ignorance about Poland' at this late stage in the proceedings, and that no attempt had been made to get his findings before the Committee.[36]

---

[31] ibid., p. 78.
[32] ibid., pp. 78–9.
[33] ibid., p. 81.

[34] ibid., pp. 81–2.
[35] ibid., p. 85.
[36] ibid., p. 83.

Ironside spent the next three days studying the papers and plans prepared by the British and French Staffs. The French had abandoned all thought of offensives, either against the Siegfried Line or against the Italians. He went to see Hore-Belisha to tell him that there were no plans, that the Germans were free to knock out Poland and Rumania, and then he went to bed 'profoundly depressed'[37] by the thought that the Prime Minister was not cut out for war; he was, in Ironside's opinion, a pacifist at heart with 'a firm belief that God has chosen him as an instrument to prevent this threatened war'.[38]

He might also have spared a thought for the Allied generals and air marshals who were not much better or different. But the Germans were singularly ignorant of this premature Allied forfeit of the Polish card. They were still greatly worried by the prospect of a war on two fronts – they had every reason to be – and they left no stone unturned to avert this fearful prospect. Late in July, at a rather dull party in Berlin, Goering himself took a hand in the operation. Once again, the chosen medium was to be the able and understanding Paul Stehlin in Berlin.

After listening to the rather boring small-talk for a little while, Stehlin recalls[39] that Goering took him aside and called Bodenschatz to join them. Goering wanted to know when the French Ambassador would be returning from his summer leave. Stehlin told him: about mid-August. 'That will be too late,' said Goering; Coulondre ought to be in Berlin; something could happen any day. Goering then impressed on Stehlin that the French Premier should be advised at once of possible developments: he should tell Daladier that France should enter no risky commitment with regard to Poland; in some three or four weeks she could find herself in a crisis far more dangerous than the pre-Munich September.

Goering arranged for Stehlin's impounded personal plane to be returned to him immediately so that he could fly to Paris

[37] ibid., p. 85.
[38] ibid., p. 83.
[39] Stehlin, pp. 200–2.

with this message. Bodenschatz added his personal warning. They would be at war with Britain and France by 1 September 'unless the Allies showed the same understanding as at Munich'. Three days later, on 31 July, Stehlin was on his way to Paris.

Next morning Stehlin was reporting to the French Air Force Commander, General Vuillemin. He gave him a detailed account of his talks with Goering and Bodenschatz, repeated his personal observation of the extent of German mobilization and his conviction that it would be completed by the middle of August; then expressed his considered view that the Germans would attack Poland within four weeks.

Vuillemin did not agree. The French government had much less pessimistic reports at its disposal, he told Stehlin; they were prepared 'for all eventualities'. This was not the issue, Stehlin answered. The question was whether Hitler could be told in precise terms just what the Allies would do in the west if the Germans attacked Poland. This was the only hope of saving the peace and Poland. But, in Stehlin's considered opinion, the Germans were probably just as well informed about French and British intentions as they were about German plans.[40] Hitler would know that the French proposed to do nothing. After this inconclusive interview, Stehlin saw the Air Minister, Guy La Chambre, for an even more frustrating exchange. Then he returned to Berlin. It was a singularly revealing interlude in the game of pre-war diplomacy.

Why did Goering intervene in this way? Was it to avert war or was it to make sure that the French kept quiet during the attack on Poland? Was he acting in collusion with Hitler in order to frighten the French and British away from the Polish front, or was he conducting an independent foreign policy? It is easier to ask these questions than to answer them; yet much depends on the correct understanding of what was taking place during these interchanges.

[40] There was, as we shall see, a curious duality in the German position. Hitler was convinced that neither the French nor the British would actively intervene during his assault on Poland, and he was right. His generals were equally convinced that the Allies would counter-attack; and they were wrong.

The central fact was that at the head of this seemingly monolithic German war machine, with its terrifying Gestapo and Himmler's Security Service to back it up, with its one party state and controlled press, with its absence of the customary democratic division, there was a personal relationship among the leaders bordering on anarchy. Intrigues and rivalries dominated the lives of Ribbentrop and Rosenberg, Goering and Goebbels, Hess and Himmler; each one of the Nazi leaders was pursuing independent policies to strengthen his own position. It was hardly better in the armed forces: the Generals were bitter and divided – even, in some important cases, defeatist. The counter-intelligence service was commanded by officers who were opposed to Hitler, seeking his overthrow and in touch with the Allies and some neutrals.

But it was Hitler's strength that at this turning point at the end of July, all his ministers and senior officers wanted the same thing, even if for different reasons. None were unduly concerned with the impending liquidation of the Polish state. What worried all of them (except Hitler himself) was the threat of Anglo-French intervention; they feared it 'for the sake of Germany'; they could not see Germany fighting a successful war on two fronts. At that party with Stehlin, Goering became their spokesman. The only way peace could be preserved was by the sacrifice of Poland, in much the same manner as Czechoslovakia was sacrificed the year before. But Goering spelled it out even more clearly. It would be France's and Britain's existence that would be at stake if they came to the aid of the Poles. Goering warned off the French because, Hitler apart, the Germans were still not convinced that the British and French would do nothing to help Poland – and the main reason for this doubt was the knowledge that the Allies in the west would enjoy tremendous military superiority during the German preoccupation with the Polish campaign in the east.

So the Germans came to London and to Paris; they came sometimes with the best of intentions, and with the worst at others; one came after the other to dissuade the British and the

French from becoming involved with their Polish ally – Trott and Kordt, Goering and Bodenschatz, and a host of others. Little did they know that Gamelin and Gort had argued their case far more effectively, and so had the British and French Air Ministers. The Germans were pushing an open door. Far from knowing all about Allied intentions, as Stehlin had assumed, the Germans were consumed with uncertainty. All the signs pointed towards Allied inaction – except one: the impressive Allied military and economic potential. The Germans could not believe that this would be left to lie fallow while they launched their assault on the Poles.

Goering, von Weizsaecker and all the others wanted to make sure of this Allied inactivity; they feared that the likely outcome of a war with Britain and France would be a crushing defeat.[41] But they had no need to worry; neither Chamberlain nor Daladier were prepared to exploit the opportunity with which Hitler had presented them; the hostage he had given them went unnoticed. Not only the two governments, but also their commanders and chiefs of staff did not know what was going on.[42] And, even worse, they *thought* they knew. Chamberlain and Daladier did not want war, and believed that Hitler did not want to go to war. Their views were reinforced by their military advisers who urged – again in ignorance of German intentions, and their self-induced fear of German armed strength – a policy of disengagement rather than commitment from the threatening Polish war.

These were critical hours for Hitler. He did not want to make the same mistake the Kaiser had made in 1914 and misread British intentions. He had repeatedly expressed his opinion to the

[41] The memoirs of the German generals and diplomats carry a considerable weight of this argument; so do the writings of the principal members of the resistance.

[42] During the critical period between March and September the Foreign Policy Committee of the Chamberlain Government – a kind of inner cabinet – met some sixty times. The FPC consisted of the hard core of Chamberlain, Halifax, Simon and Hoare, plus the Chief of the Imperial General Staff and other senior officers and Ministers, as required; see Templewood, p. 375.

generals and also to Ribbentrop that the British would not intervene if he used force against the Poles; and without British encouragement, he was certain that the French would make no hostile move. And as his hour of decision approached, more confirmation for his stand arrived – and much the most convincing evidence came from his London embassy, from the ambassador whom history and his subordinates at the time had treated as a negligible figure. But Ambassador Dirksen was not playing politics; he was not seeking to influence Hitler. He was a rather unimaginative but competent career diplomat who reported things as he found them. His reports gave Hitler that extra reassurance he needed; they complemented Seligo's report from London.

On 10 July 1939, Dirksen sent a political report to Berlin dealing with the 'stiffening mood in Britain'.[43] The report was published by the Germans after the outbreak of the war as a part of their White Book which sought to demonstrate the warmongering responsibility of the British, French and Poles. But the most significant passage in Dirksen's report, the one that must have made its greatest impact on Hitler at the time, was omitted from the German publication. Dirksen had written that the main difference between the British mood in September 1938, at the time of Munich, and 'now', in the midsummer of 1939, was that in September 1938 'the mass of the people did not want to fight and were passive'; but now they had taken the initiative and were urging the government to stand and fight. Unpleasant as the reality was, Germany would have to take note of it in a country such as Britain where 'public opinion plays so decisive a role'.

But then comes the censored part of the Dirksen dispatch, the conclusion which the Germans did not publish. It would be wrong, however, Dirksen continued, to see in this state of

[43] See Ch. 3, p. 62 above. For the most reliable account see *Documents and Materials relating to the eve of the Second World War*, vol. II (*The Dirksen Papers*) published by the Ministry of Foreign Affairs of the USSR, pp. 65–6. Also DGFP, vol. VI, pp. 892–3.

British opinion the inevitability of war. Public excitement
would calm down as soon as a quieter atmosphere in England
'would permit a more unprejudiced assessment of the German
viewpoint'. The 'germs' for such a change were already in
existence, Dirksen continued. 'Within the Cabinet and a small
influential group of politicians, a desire is manifested to pass
from the negative encirclement policy to a more constructive
attitude towards Germany ... Chamberlain's personality is a
certain guarantee that British policy will not be placed in the
hands of unscrupulous adventurers.'

Two weeks later, Dirksen reported still more encouraging
news in his account on the conversations of Dr Helmuth
Wohlthat, a special emissary of Goering's office for the Four
Year Plan, with Robert S. Hudson, the Minister for Overseas
Trade, and with Sir Horace Wilson, the Permanent Head of the
Civil Service who was Chamberlain's closest adviser in his
dealings with Germany.[44] Dirksen emphasized British disinclination to become involved with the Poles. Sir Horace had
suggested, he reported, that their objective should be a broad
Anglo-German agreement on all major questions, 'as had been
originally envisaged by the Fuehrer'. This would push such
questions as Danzig and Poland into the background. 'Sir
Horace Wilson definitely told Herr Wohlthat that the conclusion of a non-aggression pact would enable Britain to rid
herself of her commitments towards Poland, and the Polish
problem would therefore lose much of its urgency.'

But the really good news was still to come. Sir Horace told
Wohlthat that the Chamberlain government contemplated
holding a general election in the autumn.[45] Chamberlain felt
so strong that he could win whether he went to the country
on a slogan of 'preparedness for war' or for 'a lasting peace

[44] This meeting took place on 18 July. See DGFP, vol. VI, pp. 979–80;
Dirksen Papers, p. 71.

[45] On 20 July, Wohlthat had a talk with Sir George Joseph Ball, Director of
the Conservative Party's Research Department, see DGFP, vol. VI, p. 977, and
Ball confirmed that 14 November was the 'scheduled date', ibid, p. 983.

and understanding with Germany'. 'Naturally,' Sir Horace is reported to have told Herr Wohlthat, 'Chamberlain prefers the peace issue.'[46]

Wohlthat, in his personal report to Goering, had given an even more detailed account of the views expressed by Sir Horace Wilson who, in the German Ambassador's opinion, was the only man with whom Wohlthat talked whose views really mattered in assessing the British position.[47] Horace Wilson, Wohlthat reported, had come prepared for a *rapprochement* with Germany, the details of which he had set out in a 'Programme for German–British Cooperation'.[48] Sir Horace emphasized that their conversations 'must be held in secret'. Only Britain and Germany should negotiate at first; France and Italy were to be brought in later. 'The highest ranking personages' were to conduct the talks, Wohlthat reports, evidently to emphasize that these were considered quite differently to the conversations in Moscow where there were no 'ranking personages'.

After wondering whether he might be too optimistic, Horace Wilson proceeded to assess Hitler's personality, Wohlthat reports. Wilson said that he had the opportunity to observe Hitler and thought 'that the Fuehrer could, as a statesman for peace, achieve even more than he had already accomplished in the building up of Greater Germany'.[49] He believed that Hitler wanted to avert the outbreak of a world war over Danzig. Therefore, 'if the Greater Germany policy in respect of territorial claims *was approaching the end of its demands*' [my emphasis – J.K.] the Fuehrer could now proceed, in conjunction with the British government, in finding a way of doing this. Hitler would then be remembered as one of the greatest statesmen in world history and produce at the same time a revolution in world opinion regarding Germany. Wilson added that

46 *Dirksen Papers*, p. 72.
47 DGFP, vol. VI, p. 1001.
48 ibid., pp. 979–80.
49 ibid.

Chamberlain was prepared to make a similar declaration of intent. It was important, however, that such Anglo-German negotiations should 'not be brought to the knowledge of persons who were fundamentally hostile to an understanding'. Provided the British and Germans handled such talks with skill and discretion they could realize 'one of the greatest political combinations it was possible to imagine'.[50]

Wilson had, of course, stressed that the alternative to agreement would be war. But it was war in very general terms. There was, in all the talks with Wohlthat and Dirksen, not a single mention of direct British aid to Poland.[51]

However, set against everything else that Wilson had said – and a possible election in the autumn – this did not sound like mobilization for war, and Dirksen returned to the subject in yet another dispatch sent on 1 August.[52] There were more reports of conversations with British politicians favouring a settlement with Germany and Dirksen concluded that the impression was 'growing stronger and stronger' that an agreement with Germany must be arranged within a few weeks 'so that election policy can be settled'. It was hoped that the parliamentary summer recess would provide the quieter conditions necessary to the 'framing of a programme of negotiations with Germany that would have a chance of being realized'.

Two days later, on 3 August, Dirksen was again with Sir Horace Wilson.[53] This time their conversation had an added significance for it was conducted with rather more than usual frankness. Sir Horace elaborated his earlier assurance that an Anglo-German agreement would free Britain from her commitments to Poland, Turkey and other countries. This, Sir Horace

[50] ibid.

[51] For Sir Horace Wilson's version of this conversation see DBFP, vol. VI, p. 354. This gives so different an emphasis of what took place, and leaves out so many specific details mentioned by Wohlthat, that it is difficult to accept the British version as a *complete* and accurate account when compared with the separate, much fuller and seemingly independent versions given by Dirksen and Wohlthat.

[52] *Dirksen Papers*, p. 104.

[53] ibid., pp. 120–1.

explained, was conditional on the inclusion in the agreement of a renunciation of aggression towards third parties. Since such a declaration would remove the threat, there would be no need to guarantee them any longer. Wilson then elaborated on the skill and secrecy that would be necessary to bring about such an agreement before he turned to a most significant aspect of their talk. He told Dirksen that 'the British Government had information [note the date of this talk – 3 August] that two million German troops were shortly to be called to the colours; that manoeuvres menacing to Poland, with the participation of large numbers of aircraft, were to be held near the Polish frontier'.

Dirksen replied that the extensive manoeuvres planned by the Germans 'were by no means comparable to the military measures taken by other powers'. The Poles had mobilized a million men who were deployed on the German frontier ('Sir Horace questioned whether the number of Poles mobilized was so large, but offered no objection to my amended figure of 900,000')[54]; Britain's armed forces, land, sea and air, were 'more or less mobilized' and France had also taken comprehensive mobilization measures, Dirksen claimed. It was therefore not possible for the Germans 'to reverse their plans or cancel their manoeuvres'. Wilson reassured Dirksen that this was not what he had in mind. All he asked was that the manoeuvres should be conducted as was customary in peacetime. Finally, Sir Horace put three points on which the British government wanted clarification about German policy: what instructions would Hitler give to develop the closer economic relations which had been discussed with Wohlthat; would Hitler be able to ensure that the international situation would not worsen in the coming weeks; and how would Hitler make known 'his decision to take the initiative in creating an atmosphere in which the programme for the negotiations could be discussed with a prospect of success'?

It should occasion no surprise therefore if the warnings

[54] ibid., p. 121.

uttered by General Ironside during his visit to Warsaw when he told the Germans there that Britain meant to stand by Poland, fell on somewhat sceptical Nazi ears. For this was not the first example they had experienced in this context of this Anglo-French double-talk. There had been the curious interlude a few weeks earlier during which Ribbentrop had called Bonnet's bluff. But the tone which the Germans adopted towards the French was very different from the sweet reasonableness with which the Wohlthat talks were conducted in London. The exchanges with the French had begun with a Note from the French government which was handed to the German Ambassador in Paris on 1 July by the French Foreign Minister, M. Bonnet.[55] This referred back to the talks which the Foreign Minister had during Ribbentrop's visit to Paris in December 1938, and concluded with an impressively firm declaration that Bonnet regarded it as his duty 'to state definitely that any action, whatever its form, which would tend to modify the *status quo* of Danzig, and so provoke the armed resistance of Poland, would bring the Franco-Polish Agreement into play and oblige France to give immediate assistance to Poland'.

Nothing could have been clearer, nothing could have been firmer, nothing could have been more misleading and false about France's actual intentions. This was evident already from the way Bonnet had, during the visit of the Polish War Minister in May, rejected General Gamelin's much more limited undertaking. What, then, made him take this unexpectedly provocative step? Was it to impress Ribbentrop and the Germans? Bonnet must have known better. Was it to invite the kind of German response that Bonnet must have anticipated? Was he, in fact, looking for more arguments with which to counter any renewed suggestion of direct French aid to the Poles in case of a Polish conflict with Germany? We shall get our answer from the subsequent developments.

Ribbentrop had known of this intended Note (was this part of Bonnet's scenario?) and had warned the German Ambassador

[55] DGFP, vol. VI, pp. 828-9.

in Paris, Baron von Welczeck, of what he should say to Bonnet when the French Foreign Minister handed him the document.[56] Welczeck subsequently reported to Ribbentrop that he had been able to go into considerable detail in his reply to Bonnet and to warn him 'against the catastrophic policy into which France was apparently allowing herself to be drawn, in Britain's wake, under the most unfavourable circumstances'. The German added that he then proceeded to set out German military and economic strength 'in the strongest light'.

But this was only the beginning of this prepared dialogue. On 13 July, just as Wohlthat was preparing for his very different mission to London, Ribbentrop wrote a personal letter to Bonnet in Paris by way of replying to the formal Note of 1 July.[57] He also recalled their December meeting in Paris. Bonnet had then told him that a fundamental change had come about in France's attitude towards Eastern Europe as a result of the Munich Conference and that France would henceforth recognize that Eastern Europe was in the 'German sphere of interest'. This was still Germany's position. Germany's policies in the east were of no concern to France; 'accordingly, the Reich Government do not consider themselves in a position to discuss with the French Government questions of German–Polish relations, still less to admit France's right to exert any influence on questions connected with shaping the future destiny of the German city of Danzig'. And, just in case any of Bonnet's colleagues were still inclined to have doubts, Ribbentrop added that 'violation of Danzig soil by Poland, or any provocation by Poland which is incompatible with the prestige of the German Reich, would be answered by an immediate German advance and the destruction of the Polish Army'.[58]

Bonnet had the answer he had wanted. But the play was not finished. On 25 July, when he could no longer have had any doubts about France's unwillingness to launch a second front

[56] ibid.
[57] ibid, pp. 919–20.
[58] ibid.

on Poland's behalf, Bonnet replied in a personal letter to Ribbentrop.[59] It was couched in even stronger terms, asserting that France was honour bound to come to the aid of Poland, especially over the Danzig issue. If the Poles saw this letter – and Bonnet made sure they did – they must have been delighted and reassured. So was Hitler. He knew otherwise. For – in these personal exchanges with Ribbentrop – he had provided Bonnet with the instrument and the reasons he needed to make certain that there would be no effective French moves to aid the Poles.

But the politicians and diplomats were not alone in their complacent disbelief in the prospect of an early war. General Dill, Commander-in-Chief, Aldershot, and one of the ablest British generals, who was expected to be commander of the British Expeditionary Force should there be war, called at the War Office on 31 July to see General Kennedy. They talked about the prospect of war. Dill thought it unlikely that Hitler would go to war with Britain over his continental policy.[60] The danger was that 'in playing too near the precipice' he might slip over the brink.

But Hitler, as we shall see, had no such fear. Despite the warnings of his most expert advisers, of his generals, his intelligence and of the free-lance 'peace-mongers' in the German Foreign Ministry and on the General Staff, Hitler held to his position that neither the British nor the French would come to the aid of the Poles. Why was Hitler so confident in taking such a risk at a time when he had everything to lose, when he was at the peak of his power? For once he embarked on the Polish war, the cards would be decisively stacked against him for three to four weeks; he stood to lose everything if the French and British counter-attacked against his weakened western defence.

[59] ibid, pp. 1000–1.
[60] *Business of War*, pp. 12–13.

4

'But You Are the Masters'

Churchill arrived in Paris on the morning of 14 August, in the company of General Spears. They were to be the guests of the Deputy Commander-in-Chief, General Georges, and to inspect France's Maginot system of defence. As they drove through the Bois de Boulogne to a quiet lunch they could not know that at that time Hitler was briefing his Commander-in-Chief, General Brauchitsch and the Chief of Staff, General Franz Halder, on the further course of events as he proposed to shape them. But even without this insight into the conference in Hitler's study in Obersalzberg, both Churchill and Georges were certain that war was almost upon them unless the Allies once more surrendered to every German demand.[1] Both men thought that the interval since Munich had benefited the Germans; they were particularly impressed by the reports of the strength of the German Westwall, the 'Siegfried Line' along the French frontier.

On 16 August, Churchill met Gamelin who was supervising manoeuvres in the Alsace, and he returned to Paris ten days later with a feeling of considerable reassurance at the evidence provided by the French defences and, even more, by the bearing of the French armed forces.[2] In Paris, Churchill invited Georges to lunch. The French Commander came with a complete situation report; he produced details of the deployment of the

[1] Sir Edward Spears, *Assignment to Catastrophe*, vol. I, pp. 4–9.
[2] Winston S. Churchill, *The Second World War*, vol. I, p. 312.

French and German armies, and he classified the divisions according to their worth. We know now that the intelligence available to Georges about the nature of the Siegfried 'Wall', and even more so about the manning of its defences by German troops, greatly over-estimated German defensive strength at the time.[3] But even so, Churchill was impressed; he told Georges: 'But you are the Masters.'[4]

The French were the masters; even more so in fact than on the basis of the figures which so startled Churchill. They were vastly superior to the Germans on the western front on every single count. They had more than five times the number of German soldiers in the west; the French were better trained and far better equipped and supplied. They had a massive superiority in armour since there were no German tanks in the west. The French (together with the British) were considerably superior in the air, and greatly so at sea. For three weeks in September the gateways to Germany lay open to the French armies, to the RAF and the Royal Navy.

On the eve of the war, the French had approximately six million men available for military service; of these, about a million were coloured soldiers. Five million (including half a million coloured) had undergone their two years' training and had been posted: 2,800,000 to front line units and 1,925,000 to the home front; the remainder had not been allocated.[5] A considerable part of this great storehouse of manpower had been mobilized through the summer and held in the more sensitive defence areas, but even so, the French High Command did not wait for the outbreak of war before it began to mobilize in earnest.

The French system of formal mobilization proceeded by stages which, in fact, resulted in a mobilization of something like three quarters of all men *before* the general mobilization was

[3] ibid., p. 300; General Gauché, *Le Deuxième Bureau au Travail*, pp. 162–5; Liss, p. 87.

[4] Churchill, p. 312.

[5] The French have been curiously reticent in making official details available, but the Germans captured most relevant French papers when they occupied Paris and were able to use them to confirm their earlier estimates; see Liss, p. 25.

proclaimed. This happened in August 1939. The first of the four periods, the 'tension-stage', was already in operation during the summer. This 'Stage One', known as the *alerte* called up the active sections of forty-nine special fortress battalions and of forty-three picked artillery units. It also prepared the country for further mobilization measures; offices and depots were made ready for the next steps.

On 21 August, Gamelin informed Hore-Belisha,[6] that French mobilization was under way. On that day the air defence system (*'réduit'*) was put into operation; on the next day – 22 August – came 'Stage Two' of the pre-mobilization, *alerte renforcée*. This, too, was largely a formality. The troops were already in position and 'Stage Three' with its special measures for the security of Paris and of the more exposed north-east and south-east 'gateways' to France followed at once. So did the completion of the air defence measures. On 24 August, came the significant 'Stage Four', the *couverture*. At first, it was applied only to the frontier areas, but on 26 August, it was extended to all France.[7]

German intelligence noted later, when after the occupation of Paris they were able to study the relevant French papers, that French mobilization was way ahead of the Germans and had been prepared, in fact, over a considerable period. By 26 August, the French had actually mobilized three quarters of their armed forces – seventy-two divisions in all, and they had not yet proclaimed a state of general mobilization. This they did on 1 September. Fully mobilized, the French had assembled ninety-nine divisions and 11,000 guns in Metropolitan France.[8] The French forces had 3,286 tanks, of which six hundred were rather obsolete Renault FT light tanks.[9]

[6] R. J. Minney, *The Private Papers of Hore-Belisha*, p. 215.

[7] See Liss, pp. 41 and 84.

[8] Gamelin, vol. III, pp. 34–6.

[9] Many conflicting estimates and totals have been given by French sources. German intelligence initially greatly overestimated French armour; it credited the French with 4,535 tanks, but this was later revised in the light of captured documents. See Liss, p. 269; P. Tissier, *The Riom Trial*, p. 51; and Gamelin, *passim*.

Confusion and conflict surround official French accounts by
Ministers and Senior Officers, especially at the Riom Trial
which was designed to establish the guilt of the Popular Front,
about the actual strength of the French Air Force. German
intelligence estimates were again not much help as these also
over-estimated the availability of serviceable French aircraft.
On 1 September, the French had in fact 463 first line, though
not very modern, bomber aircraft and 634 first line fighters.
But to give an effective picture of the situation, we must add to
these 566 British bombers and 608 fighters, a total of approximately 2,200 bombers and fighters[10] against Germany's 3,600
of which, however, 2,600 were engaged in Poland.

But the most important factor which emerges from this
summary is that this great array of force was assembled and
ready for action by the end of the first week of September,
even if we count no more than those mobilized by 26 August:
seventy-two divisions, 8,000 guns, 2,500 tanks and 2,000 first
line aircraft; four million men were in position, the men
Churchill described as 'the masters'. What kind of opposition
did they have to face on the morning of 9 September, fourteen
days after mobilization; what kind of opposition would they
have found had they proceeded to attack the German lines in
order to relieve the hard-pressed Poles?

After months of fearful speculation and intelligence, the
French and British Allies were at last face to face with the
German reality. But the 'psychological block' to which Churchill
had referred[11] was still at work. The '*Bulletin de Renseigne-
ments*' of the *Deuxième Bureau* for 9 September, circulated the
latest French intelligence about the German forces in the west.
The *Deuxième Bureau* reported that there were forty-three
German divisions along the Westwall, and it placed and
identified twenty-six of them.[12] It had previously, at the outbreak

---

[10] *Strategy*, p. 33; these figures are roughly the same as those arrived at by
Tissier after studying the Riom Trial evidence.

[11] Churchill, p. 300.

[12] Liss, p. 87; Gauché, pp. 163–5.

D

of the war, indicated that Germany had mobilized 135 divisions,[13] and it had credited the German Air Force and armoured units with a considerable excess of aircraft and tanks over the more sober reality.

On that same morning of 9 September, a Saturday, on which the French intelligence service circulated its revised estimate to the army commanders and the government, the German Chief of Staff of the Army, Maj.-General Halder, prepared a detailed situation map of the western front for submission to Hitler after receiving a report from his Intelligence Chief, Admiral Canaris, that the French were about to attack the Saar.[14] Halder was becoming increasingly worried. He could not understand the French inactivity in the west, and his puzzlement is easier to understand than the passivity of the French when we turn to his map,[15] revised now to include the actual number of the French divisions and not only those assumed to be there by the German intelligence.

Facing the four-and-a-half million French were some 800,000 Germans; but approximately half of these were still in the process of assembly, or on their way to the front. As he studied his situation map that day, Halder began to understand the enormity of the risk Hitler was taking, and what he had meant when he had spoken of the '*Risiko*' which was an inevitable part of their operations plan.

The picture was a little better than it had been at the outbreak of the war but it was still far from reassuring, and Halder was painfully aware that his paper markers on the map hardly reflected the real situation on the ground. Thus, confronting the seventy-two French divisions, the élite of the French, was the German Army Group C under von Leeb, one of Germany's outstanding generals, reputed for his knowledge of defensive war. He had taken over command from General von Witzleben at his Frankfurt headquarters, on the outbreak of war, and

[13] They had only ninety at the most optimistic count, see Liss, p. 87.
[14] See Jodl's evidence in *Trial of Major War Criminals*, vol. XV, p. 373.
[15] Halder, *Kriegstagebuch*, vol. I, Map 1.

Witzleben's parting briefing caused von Leeb to make his own survey of the situation.[16] Von Witzleben's view was that, as things were, if the French were to attack they would break through the German lines.[17]

After reviewing his troops and dispositions, von Leeb realized that von Witzleben had not exaggerated. On 2 September, he sent a courier to the Supreme Commander, General von Brauchitsch, at headquarters in Berlin with a strictly confidential account of the alarming state of his front, especially that part covering a possible allied advance through Belgium and Holland. Altogether, he said, he had there only two *Landwehr* divisions (third line Home Guard units), one First Line regiment and two Fourth Line replacement divisions which still had to be trained. There were also some frontier security forces.

The position was such that one of the Home Guard divisions, the 225th, had to man a front of fifty miles, and the two untrained Fourth Line Divisions had an eighty-mile sector to look after. He could not see the French remaining idle under such conditions and he asked urgently for additional reserve units, especially as it would take six days before these could reach their positions at the front. His immediate concern was the likelihood of a French attack and the unlikely probability that it could be halted at the German frontier. He speculated no further.[18]

A week had passed since von Leeb's appeal when Halder prepared his map on 9 September.[19] Von Leeb's Army still had not a single tank and only a few aircraft. On paper, at least, he now had a hard core of fifteen First Line, 'active' – as the Germans called them – divisions; these were backed by eleven *Landwehr* (Home Guard) divisions composed largely of men

---

[16] Von Witzleben's – and subsequently von Leeb's – accounts of the state of the western front were also confirmed by General von Lossberg, deputy-operations officer at the Fuehrer's HQ; see his *Im Wehrmacht-Fuehrungsstab*, p. 36.

[17] H. B. Gisevius, *To the Bitter End*, p. 359.

[18] H. A. Jacobsen, ed., *Dokumente zur Vorgeschichte des Westfeldzuges 1939–1940*, pp. 74–5.

[19] Halder, *Kriegstagebuch*, vol. I, Map 1.

over thirty and of officers from the first world war, and by seven Fourth Line divisions, in fact only partly-trained replacement units. The army had only limited petrol and ammunition supplies. General Westphal has estimated that they would not have been sufficient to fight a three days' war.[20]

Altogether, General Halder listed forty divisions which, in theory, were available to von Leeb. But many of these still required time, a week or much more, before they could be committed to battle. And, if anything, Halder realized that the strategic threat was even greater than that produced by the German numerical inferiority in the overall situation. Hitler had put all his eggs into the central sector of the front; the north and south were only thinly protected. This type of disposition could easily become a trap for the Germans; but Hitler remained confident that there would be no Allied attack.

Thus von Leeb had only one First Line division and six indifferent others to protect the northern approaches through Belgium; three First Line and seven other divisions covered the vulnerable Luxemburg–Moselle gap; the bulk of his force was stationed in the best prepared part of the Siegfried Wall, on the Saar front down to the Rhine bend at Karlsruhe – eight First Line divisions and nine others (and it was this forward concentration which particularly worried Halder; it could so easily be outflanked). Two First Line divisions and four others were all that was left for the Upper Rhine and Black Forest sector down to the Swiss frontier at Basle.

Halder's map, it turned out, was more of an expression of hope than a statement of fact on the morning of 9 September. Von Leeb's Army Group C, as we have seen, had no armour to back it and virtually no aircraft to protect it. A minimum of First Line aircraft had been held back from the Polish front as cover for German cities against possible British air attacks, but hardly any were made available for the western front.

This imbalance of the German forces was reflected in the

[20] Siegfried Westphal, *Heer in Fesseln*, p. 112.

figures which General Georges had shown to Churchill in Paris on 26 August,[21] and Churchill had passed them to Hore-Belisha two days later,[22] immediately after his return to London. Hore-Belisha advised the Cabinet on 30 August that he had information that the Germans had fifteen divisions on the western front and forty-six in Poland.[23] It was a fairly accurate estimate of the number of German troops that were actually ready on the eve of the attack on Poland – and it emphasizes the critical importance of these first days of the war.

German accounts of the size of their force in the west have varied considerably, but this was largely due to the different periods which were described but never specified. Thus there was a considerable margin between the number of German troops in the west at the beginning of the war with Poland, during the first ten days of September, and the end of the Polish campaign, during the last week of September. It was the early September days that mattered.

During his interrogation after the war, the man who ought to know best, General Jodl, claimed that there were no more than twenty-three divisions in the west at the beginning of the war.[24] General Westphal, who commanded a reserve division in the west and who has given the most detailed and convincing account of the state of the front, maintained that, after assembly had been completed (he gives no precise date), the Germans had eight First Line and twenty-five other, largely indifferent, divisions to man the Westwall – a total of thirty-three divisions.[25] The British official historian, with access to all available evidence, has come to the same conclusion.[26] General von Manstein calculated that there were eleven First Line divisions and thirty-six others (but of these, he says thirty-four were only partially serviceable); he appears, however, to be writing on the

[21] See above, p. 87.
[22] *Belisha Papers*, p. 222.
[23] ibid., p. 223.
[24] *Trial of Major War Criminals*, vol. XV, p. 385.
[25] Westphal, pp. 109–11.
[26] *Strategy*, p. 60.

state of the front about the middle of September, not at the beginning of the war.[27]

Telford Taylor, one of the American prosecuting counsel at Nuremberg, bases himself on an earlier Halder estimate to reach conclusions that seem particularly wide of the mark – he comes to the conclusion that there was virtually a balance of forces on the western front.[28] But with the added information now at our disposal we may deal with certainties and not with speculation: during the decisive first weeks of September, as we have seen, the Allies enjoyed a degree of superiority and a strategic opportunity such as never again presented itself during the course of the war.[29]

Moreover, the Allied military superiority in the west was further emphasized by the incomplete and inadequate character of the Siegfried Line. Despite desperate last-minute attempts to repair some of the worst omissions,[30] such as the absence of turrets and adequate shutters and machine-gun mounts, as well as other essential equipment, the basic fact remained that the 'Line' as such was little more than a 'Potemkin Village', as General Westphal described its condition when his reserve unit reached its station at the outbreak of the war.

The Westwall was an altogether curious affair. It had been outwardly completed at some key positions, especially in the Saar, but elsewhere only the first line of defence had been finished – and in many places not even that. There was no system allowing defence in depth; there was no adequate shelter for the troops if they were exposed to air or heavy artillery attack. Even in August and September there were still over 150,000 mostly foreign workers engaged in construction work.

There was yet another burden which befell the German army in the west. The German transport system could not cope with

27 Erich von Manstein, *Verlorene Siege*, pp. 24–5; the translation of this passage is not altogether accurate in the English edition.

28 Telford Taylor, *Sword and Swastika*, p. 296.

29 See Liss, *passim*.

30 Westphal, pp. 116–7. Telford Taylor, p. 272; author's personal interviews with German officers serving in Westwall positions at the time.

the simultaneous demands of the mobilization against Poland and in the west. Priority was given to the requirements of the eastern front and units and transport to the west were accordingly seriously delayed. It took General Westphal's reserve unit a full ten days to assemble and move to its position in the Siegfried Line.[31] Colonel Gercke, the chief of the Transport Section of the Army General Staff, advised his superiors that the railways were in no position to cope with all the requirements; he estimated that it would take a division thirteen days from the time of its mobilization until it reached its scheduled position on the western front.[32] Von Leeb, as we have seen,[33] told Brauchitsch that it took six days for assembled divisions to reach the front.

With this knowledge of the actual forces which confronted each other in the west, and of the additional advantages which favoured the French and British to such an inordinate extent, we can turn back now to the unsuspectingly decisive days of August and conclude our investigation into the circumstances – and responsibilities – which led to the failure of the Anglo-French alliance to fight the one battle that would have finished the war – and probably also Hitler – in the autumn of 1939.

We must turn back to 14 August, the day Churchill arrived in Paris for his revealing lunch with General Georges. For about the same time, the German Army Commander von Brauchitsch, the Chief of Staff Halder, the Navy and Luftwaffe Commanders Raeder and Goering, and the principal architect and engineer of the Westwall, Dr Todt, were on their way to Obersalzberg. They had been summoned by Hitler for a special briefing. Yet there has been curiously little attention paid by the historians to this – considering its timing – decisive meeting between Hitler and his inner circle of senior army officers. Moreover, it has been further discounted by emphasis on the similarities of Hitler's 14 August exposition with those he made

[31] Westphal, p. 110.
[32] Telford Taylor, p. 272.
[33] See p 91. above.

to Count Ciano on the two previous days. Yet the real significance lay not in the similarities of the two briefings but in their fundamental differences. Each, in turn, was a part of Hitler's unfolding pattern.

It was not, however, the pattern of a free mind, or of a great leader who makes his choice between a number of possible options. Hitler, for all his power, was not in that fortunate position. He could not wait for the pattern to unfold. He had to make things happen. He was a prisoner of his own design. It had to be complete by 1 September. *So oder so*, the Danzig and Polish questions had to be settled. And by the beginning of August, it was clear to him that there could no longer be a peaceful conclusion of the Polish crisis on any terms other than complete Polish submission. It was also becoming clear that it was no longer necessary to consider a peaceful settlement with Poland. The talks with the Russians had advanced sufficiently to reassure Hitler that *given time* he would reach an agreement with Stalin. But since time was the one thing he could not afford, he would have to pay a price for the Russian deal. He was clear in his mind that there was only one possible offer that he could make which would be acceptable to Stalin: Eastern Poland. This, then, was further reason for his conviction that a settlement of the Polish question by force was not only inevitable but also desirable. Anything else would disrupt his timetable and ruin his pattern.

Something else, hardly less important, had become clear to him by the early days of August. The reports which he had received from the ambassador in London, from Dr Wohlthat on his return, and from a variety of other sources, convinced him for the moment of one central factor in his equation: whatever the British would do, whether they would plump for another Munich or go to war against Germany, they were not thinking of taking immediate offensive action against Germany in order to exploit Germany's preoccupation on the Polish front. The same applied to the French. This, as he saw it, was a weak link in his plans: for his concept of the proposed pact with the

Soviet Union combined with the 'settlement' of the Polish question could be ruined through a premature peace initiative by either Mussolini or Chamberlain. The second weak link of his plan was that if his information and assumptions were mistaken, an Anglo-French offensive in the west would jeopardize the swift conclusion of the Polish war and even threaten the security of the Reich. Hitler was thus fully conscious of his '*Risiko*'; the risks were tremendous and the time was desperately short – barely ten days to 26 August, his preferred date for the attack on Poland. He decided to take personal charge of events.

We know that Hitler knew that Ciano was regularly passing information to the British, especially details concerning German intentions. Pressure from Rome for another meeting between Hitler and Mussolini provided an opportunity for which Hitler had been looking. The encounter with Mussolini was sidetracked but the Italians were encouraged to send Ciano to see Ribbentrop instead. Arrangements were made, however, that after meeting with Ribbentrop, Ciano was to be briefed by Hitler in person. Mussolini and Ciano were, moreover, to be encouraged to believe that the main topic for Ciano's talks was Italy's participation in a war 'forced on Germany'. Yet this was the one point that least interested Hitler at this moment: his objectives for the talks with Ciano were twofold: to stifle at birth any thought of a conference initiated by Mussolini and designed to bring about the peaceful settlement of the Polish question, and to set up Ciano as a pipeline for information which Hitler wanted to have passed to the British without either Ciano or the British being aware of the manoeuvre. Ciano was to be used to plant information on the British which would strengthen their opposition to an immediate military intervention on the western front, and at the same time discourage Chamberlain from any further attempts at mediation. Thus, the stage was set at Obersalzberg.[34]

[34] See DGFP, vol. VII, p. 32, (Note: all references to vol. VII are to the German edition); Walter Goerlitz, *Keitel – Verbrecher oder Offizier*, pp. 210–11; F. Halder, *Kriegstagebuch*, vol. I, p. 15.

After spending 11 August with Ribbentrop, Ciano came to Obersalzberg on 12 August, a Saturday, and again on the Sunday.[35] He had two lengthy talks with the Fuehrer during which Hitler did most of the talking. Clearly embedded in his presentation – almost too clearly – was the message Hitler intended for the British and the French, and, as we know, Ciano unsuspectingly obliged,[36] but only in a somewhat diluted form.[37]

Hitler began with a description of the situation on Germany's western front and, with the aid of faked maps spread on the table, proceeded to give Ciano a situation report which was false on virtually every count that mattered most to Britain and France. Hitler emphasized the great strength of the German fortifications in the west and elaborated on non-existent details which would frustrate any French attempt to overrun the Siegfried Line along the traditional gateways of attack. He made a particular point of emphasizing the massiveness of the German defences along the Belgian border where, in fact, they were exceptionally weak and incomplete.[38]

Next, Hitler played on the known fears of the British government and the Air Ministry. Any attempt to blockade Germany would be met by counter-attack from the air; all of England, Hitler added, was now within the striking distance of the new German bombers, a fact which was mistakenly later interpreted by the Air Staff in London as an indication that the Luftwaffe had in fact a strategic bomber force capable of launching independent air raids on Britain's principal cities.[39] Hitler appeared to be fully aware of this sensitive area in British defence thinking, and he played on it from every possible angle. Thus he returned to the subject immediately he began to discuss military relationship of the Allies to Poland. The central factor was the exposure of Britain to injury from the air. London

[35] *Ciano Diaries*, pp. 124–6; E. Wiskemann, *Rome-Berlin Axis*.

[36] *Ciano Diaries*, p. 125; DGFP, vol. VII, p. 32; Sir Ivone Kirkpatrick *Mussolini*, pp. 394–6.

[37] See pp. 99–100 below.

[38] DGFP, vol. VII, pp. 33–4.

[39] See *Strategy*, p. 17.

could be attacked from great heights without interference from the anti-aircraft defences, he explained to Ciano; and, with his eyes firmly fixed on Chamberlain rather than Mussolini, he added that the RAF would not be able to spare many fighters for the French front as he intended to attack Britain with his air fleets immediately on the outbreak of the war. The British would need every available fighter plane for their own defence.[40]

This was Hitler's message for Ciano. He gave him no opportunity of misunderstanding the implications. There would be war against Poland, and an immediate massive attack on Britain if she decided to join the contest. Yet every single factor mentioned by Hitler in this catalogue of German strength was either untrue or non-existent – just like the description of the Siegfried Line. The Luftwaffe had no strategic bomber force. The German so-called twin-engined bomber was geared to operating with the land armies, not in independent operations. The Luftwaffe had neither the means – the aircraft and the bombs – that could have attacked London at the outbreak of war on any sizeable scale, nor any plans to do so. But Ciano did not know that. He came away impressed by the German determination to go to war and by the military capacity she could muster on land and in the air in support of the attack against Poland and, if need be, against Poland's allies. They met again on the following day, Sunday. Hitler made the same points again but stressing the absolute determination to have done with Poland. She would be so crushed as to cease to be a military factor for another decade. Under such conditions he could take issue with the Western Allies.[41]

Ciano returned to Rome and prepared a full report on his talks for Mussolini. But he somewhat changed Hitler's emphasis. For the Fuehrer had said something in passing, it was more of an aside to which Hitler gave no undue emphasis, but which had roused Ciano's suspicion.[42] Hitler had said,

[40] DGFP, vol. VII, pp. 44–5.
[41] ibid.
[42] ibid, p. 34.

in the course of his Saturday exposition, that the French
would be no more able to overrun the German lines than they
could break through the Italian frontier defences. Hitler had
brushed aside Ciano's interjection of doubt as of no consequence. But to Ciano – and Mussolini – this was everything;
this they knew. The Italians were convinced that they were in
no condition to halt a French advance into Italy, and Hitler's
inability or unwillingness to appreciate the significance of this
Italian inferiority made Ciano doubt Hitler's judgement on the
other assessments Hitler had made during their talks. It was this,
then, that preoccupied Ciano far more than all the planted
information that Hitler had wanted him to pass on to the
English and the French. It was one of Hitler's rare errors of
judgement in the handling of his allies – and it was one that
carried fateful consequences. It frightened Mussolini. It reinforced his inclination to stay out of the war – and it also
devalued much of the information which was intended for the
French and British, the picture of invincible German strength.

   In the event it did not matter much either way; for the Allies
reached the conclusions which Hitler wanted them to accept
even without Ciano's assistance. The one thing the British and
the French governments never considered for one moment in
all their talks and conferences was the possibility of coming to
the aid of the Poles while they were under attack. Hitler clearly
was aware of that; and this was all that mattered to him. This
he proceeded to explain to his senior commanders when they
assembled in his study on Monday morning, the day after
Ciano's departure – 14 August.[43] He could not tell them stories
about the Westwall, or about the strength of the Germans in the
west and the massive attacks which the Luftwaffe would mount
against the cities of France and Britain, as he had done with
Ciano. The time had come to face realities, it was time for the
decision; only twelve days before the armies were scheduled to
march and Hitler and these men in his study knew the reality of
the balance of power in the west. The essence of Hitler's theme,

[43] DGFP, vol. VII, pp. 461–6; Halder, pp. 8–14.

therefore, was very different from that with which he sought to impress Ciano.

He began by admitting that there could be neither political nor military success without a considerable element of risk. He coolly and factually reviewed the state of the neutrals, the uncertain and the probable enemies of Germany, but he said nothing at all about the German position; not a word about the strength of her defences in the west or of the offensive capacity of the Luftwaffe. These men knew all about that. Instead, he spoke as if he was fully in the picture about British and French intentions. He explained why, if he were in Chamberlain's or Daladier's boots, he would not take the responsibility of going to war. He reassured the generals. There were no preparations for an all-out offensive against Germany: the 'men of Munich' were not prepared to take risks, and both the British and French General Staff had made sober assessments and advised against going to war.[44] The British, he concluded, were not serious with their guarantee to the Poles. Intercepted telephone conversations had provided Hitler with confirmatory evidence.

What concerned him most at that moment, Hitler told his inner circle, was that the British might attempt to interfere with the final solution of the Polish question by making new compromise proposals for a settlement. Germany, therefore, had to proceed with the total isolation of the Poles while not ignoring the possibility of having to fight also in the west. He said enough to convey to his audience that an understanding with the Russians was under way and that the Russians appreciated the need for the beating down of the Poles by force. But it was essential that the Germans achieved measurable successes within the first eight to fourteen days of the fighting in Poland. It was most important, therefore, that the rest of the world should come to understand that a solution by force was inevitable under all circumstances and that the Polish question

[44] For confirmation of the accuracy of Hitler's estimate see Sir John Slessor's account of the Anglo-French staff talks in which he represented the RAF: *The Central Blue*, pp. 214–30.

would be settled in six to eight weeks – even if the English declared war, Hitler concluded.

Hitler and the Generals met again in the afternoon. For the first time, Hitler referred to the limitations of German strength in the west. They had to husband their forces and not engage in even minor encounters. He urged the army commanders to find out what other possible reserves were available and to advance the timetable for the movement of troops into the western positions. But he gave no details. He remained confident that there would be no serious attack by the French because the British were not willing to back it. In fact, the British had put out feelers, Hitler added, to find out how he saw the further developments after the fall of Poland. Even prominent British politicians who had urged a firm stand against Germany were beginning to retreat and to shelter 'behind the Ironside report' that the Polish army was no match for the Germans, Hitler assured them.

Early the following morning, General Halder met with the State Secretary of the Foreign Ministry, von Weizsaecker.[45] Halder gave him a summary of Hitler's briefing and von Weizsaecker confirmed the accuracy of Hitler's assessment of the world situation. In particular, von Weizsaecker emphasized the anxiety of Chamberlain and Halifax to avoid shedding blood. Moreover, the Americans were evidently holding back. In general, von Weizsaecker agreed with Hitler's appraisal of the likely course of events for the coming ten days. This conversation took place before nine o'clock on Tuesday 15 August.[46]

A little later that same morning, the former German ambassador to Italy, Ulrich von Hassell, one of the most determined members of the group opposing Hitler, called on the British Ambassador, Sir Neville Henderson.[47] They discussed Ciano's

---

[45] Von Weizsaecker had a 'betting box' in his office and still laid odds on peace; see Lossberg, pp. 29–30.

[46] Halder, p. 15.

[47] *Hassell Diaries*, pp. 60–1.

visit to Salzburg but were evidently unacquainted with any details. Henderson sounded fairly pessimistic and thought the odds were on war. Von Hassell did not stay long and returned home.

Later that afternoon, Gisevius came to von Hassell 'in great excitement'.[48] He gave von Hassell an accurate summary of what Hitler had told the army commanders at Obersalzberg. As a result, he said, the Nuremberg Party Rally had been called off and preparations were under way in Upper Silesia to provoke the Poles in a manner that would make war inevitable. Gisevius added the further information that Hitler did not believe that the Western Powers would intervene, but that he was ready for them if they did. However, the news which shocked von Hassell most was Gisevius' report of the imminence of a German agreement with the Soviet Union.

It is evident now that Gisevius must have received this information from von Weizsaecker, either directly or through Erich Kordt. It was the most important piece of information that had yet reached Hitler's opponents. Von Hassell consulted immediately with Goerdeler, and Gisevius told other leading members of the 'resistance'. By that evening all the principals of the opposition were fully informed of Hitler's detailed plans, especially that the die had been cast for war, no matter what happened.

Here we come to the first critical moment of the battle that was not fought. We have no direct evidence that the information concerning the 14 August conference at Obersalzberg and the decisions taken there, was passed on to either the British or French embassies, or to their service attachés. But we must assume that a man like von Hassell who had been in touch on every issue with Henderson, or Kordt, Oster, or Gisevius himself, who had regular contact with the Western Allies, would not have failed to convey so vital an item of information. But the fact remains that insofar as it has been possible to check, neither the Foreign Office nor the War Office was advised on

[48] ibid.

15 August, or thereabouts, that Hitler had made his decision to go to war – the one decision that mattered more than all others. There is no record of it having been noted either by the Cabinet or the Foreign Policy Committee of the Cabinet; the Imperial General Staff was certainly not aware of it.

The British Ambassador in Berlin, Sir Neville Henderson, was evidently not told anything about this decision by his German friends who shared his anxiety to preserve the peace, and who had sustained him all along in his efforts to bring about a last-minute mediation by Chamberlain which would compel the Poles to accept Germany's minimal terms. For on 16 August – two days after the Obersalzberg briefing – Henderson wrote a long personal letter to William Strang at the Foreign Office.[49] It was franker, more considered and more personal than the normal run of Henderson's dispatches, and it contains one telling paragraph which shows that Henderson could have had no inkling of the Obersalzberg decisions when he wrote that letter. (Even much later, when Henderson wrote his memoirs after the outbreak of the war, he had no knowledge of Hitler's 14 August briefing.[50])

Referring to a précis of the conversation which Hitler had with the Swiss High Commissioner for Danzig on 11 August (the day before Hitler talked with Ciano), Henderson writes that he is convinced that 'Hitler was speaking the truth when he spoke about holding the generals back this year. Of all Germans, believe it or not, Hitler is the most moderate as far as Danzig and the Corridor are concerned.'[51] No man who had knowledge of the Obersalzberg talks could have written that.[52]

We come therefore to the second puzzle about the 14 August conference at Obersalzberg. Could it be that the resistance leaders decided not to inform the British and French – and

[49] DBFP, vol. VII, p. 38.

[50] See Henderson, p. 253.

[51] DBFP, vol. VII, p. 37.

[52] In his *Failure of a Mission*, Henderson puts a quite different slant on his reporting at that time, one that is not borne out by his dispatches, ibid., pp. 252–30.

certainly not the Poles – that the irrevocable decision to go to war against Poland had been taken? Could it be that they saw the last hope for a peaceful settlement disappear if they advised Chamberlain that neither mediation nor a conference would prevent war breaking out? Could it be that they preferred to accept Hitler's reasoning that a swift destruction of Poland would be followed by a generous peace offer to Britain and France rather than face the only other realistic alternative?

For the one alternative that was still possible immediately after 14 August was to inform the British of the decision taken at Obersalzberg and of the nakedness of the German defences in the west – the opportunity for an Allied counter-offensive across the Rhine and from the air. It meant, in short, ensuring a German military defeat in the west while the bulk of the German forces were fully engaged in the east. But to make this possible, the French and the British would have to begin their mobilization at once. They were not told, and they did not mobilize on the morrow of 14 August.[53]

The reason for this evident silence and acquiescence in Hitler's plan was given by General Halder in a memorandum to the Commission of Investigation[54] of the German Bundestag after the war. He was giving written evidence concerning the attitude of the opponents of Hitler in general and of Dr von Etzdorf, later German Ambassador in London, in particular. He referred to a memorandum which von Etzdorf had prepared in the autumn of 1939, but what Halder said clearly applied equally to the stand taken by the resistance leaders after the Obersalzberg decisions of 14 August. Halder wrote[55] that 'in the same way as Baron von Weizsaecker and the High Command of the Army, so did Herr von Etzdorf

[53] German mobilization began in secret on 18 August, and was made formal on 25 August; see B. Mueller-Hillebrand, *Das Heer*, vol. II, p. 16.

[54] Among the members of the Inquiry Commission were Eugen Gerstenmaier and Fritz Erler. Halder's statement and the Etzdorf memorandum are reproduced in the Report of the Commission; see *Deutscher Bundestag, Erste Wahlperiode*, Drucksache No. 3465, 1949.

[55] ibid., p. 57.

recognize the impassable limit of all active resistance to Hitler: it must not lead to handicapping or obstruction of the troops engaged in battle. We never even thought of acts of sabotage; on the contrary, we were united in the conviction that the unshakeable maintenance of the German front was an essential prerequisite if there were to be negotiable peace talks.'

The concept of deliberately bringing about a German defeat was wholly alien to the German generals. It was all the more so, as long as the issue was Poland and not Britain or France. The idea of the 'back-lash' which Gisevius advocated implied risking a controlled and limited defeat by the French and British which would lead to the overthrow of Hitler by the German army.[56] Halder, and also Oster, turned this down before the attack on Poland; it was considered only as a possibly lesser evil to a *total* defeat of Germany by the Western Powers, and, indeed, later in 1944 it was accepted as the lesser evil to defeat by the Russians. But the issue did not arise on the eve of the projected war against Poland in September 1939.

All of which may explain why the German resistance leaders failed to advise the British and French of Hitler's determination to use force against Poland; it does not explain how the British and French secret services failed to obtain this precise information in time through their own channels. But whatever the reason, neither the Allied diplomats, nor their service attachés, nor even their intelligence service, were aware of the encounter at Obersalzberg. 14 August passed unnoticed in Paris and London. The most precious week in the history of modern Europe was thus lost. France did not begin with the first of her four stages of pre-mobilization until 21 August.[57]

Halder had started on the morning of 15 August. After his talk with von Weizsaecker, he began issuing wide-ranging orders which flowed from the decision at Obersalzberg. He ordered the army commanders to come and see him in turn so as to be briefed in person; he arranged for the transfer

[56] Gisevius, p. 375.
[57] See Liss, p. 84.

of the High Command to its war headquarters; he ordered the withdrawal of the civilian labour units from the advanced positions in the west, and he set in train a hundred and one other operations that were to put the armed forces on a complete war footing in time to strike at Poland on 26 August.[58]

These preparations assumed dimensions that could no longer be hidden from either the Polish or the Anglo-French secret services. They were accurately informed of the assembly of German troops which had begun well ahead of any formal attack. 25 August as 'Zero hour' was as openly mentioned in Allied diplomatic dispatches as if the Germans had made a public announcement of their intention.[59]

But neither Chamberlain nor his military advisers believed that Hitler would go through with it. The missing link in their information was Hitler's political argumentation of 14 August. They were quite sure that Hitler was bluffing. The British were convinced that the risk of a world war would, at the last moment, deter Hitler from attacking the Poles.

There was, however, one vital element absent in Chamberlain's deterrent – or it might have worked. Because of this, Chamberlain's intended deterrent became in effect an encouragement for Hitler; it was the one point where both agreed, where Chamberlain (and Daladier) did just what Hitler wanted them to do: they made no attempt at any immediate intervention in the war. They stood aside while Hitler overran Poland – in fact, in the twenty days before war broke out, the British government almost demonstratively indicated its lack of interest in halting the inexorable march of fate as far as Poland was concerned. Chamberlain was sure that Hitler did not want war – and vetoed all advance war preparations by the Chiefs of Staff.[60]

[58] Halder, pp. 15–17.
[59] See letter from Halifax to Chamberlain dated 19 Aug., DBFP, vol. VII, p. 81.
[60] See *Belisha Papers*, pp. 215–25.

Immediately, after Hitler had spoken with Burckhardt (on the Friday), with Ciano on the Saturday and Sunday, and with Halder and his commanders on the Monday – 14 August – German attention was focused on British reaction. It was known that Burckhardt would report to Halifax, it was assumed that Ciano would inform the British, and it was expected that British intelligence would hear of Hitler's decision to resort to force. But nothing happened. Parliament had recessed on 4 August. Chamberlain went off on a fishing holiday and Hore-Belisha to the South of France. Halifax also departed. The Germans were inclined to be suspicious; this looked too much like an elaborate deception to calm their fears. But Hitler evidently had been reassured; this was genuine British unconcern. The British might declare war if Hitler attacked the Poles; that was still on the cards. But there were no psychological or physical preparations for swift action either by the French or the RAF.[61] On the contrary, the Anglo-French Joint Staff was working, on Gamelin's initiative, on something which he described as non-provocative warfare.[62] The British and French would do nothing that would invite German counter-action or retaliation.

Chamberlain was most concerned that the Cabinet should accept this position and in order to impress on the doubters the seriousness of this possibility he 'corrected' the estimates of the Luftwaffe prepared by the RAF intelligence section. The figures of the Luftwaffe's establishment which Chamberlain submitted to the Cabinet were twice as large as those which Air Intelligence had given him.[63] We have Chamberlain's own account of his conviction that the secret talks which were going on at this time with Hitler and Goering looked most promising to him. Chamberlain believed that Hitler 'did seriously con-

[61] See the relevant accounts in *Belisha Papers; Ironside Diaries*; Slessor. See also *Strategy*, pp. 56–7.

[62] *Strategy*, p. 57.

[63] The source for this charge is quite unimpeachable but cannot be named. The facts of the case have been carefully checked and confirmed by senior officers concerned with the incident.

template an agreement with us'[64] and that he had seriously worked at proposals which to Hitler had seemed fabulously generous. No shadow of information about Hitler's Obersalzberg decision darkened Chamberlain's fishing holiday before he returned for the Cabinet meeting on 22 August.

Halifax had written to him on 19 August – as we have seen – that he had reliable information that the German attack would be launched on the 25th and that therefore there was no time to lose. Quite correctly, Halifax continued to tell the Prime Minister, there were indications[65] 'that Herr Hitler still believes that we do not mean to fight, or that alternatively, he can crush Poland before we can come in'. Halifax wondered whether any further British declarations of intent would serve any purpose since Hitler clearly did not believe them. All the same, he proposed to discuss with the British Ambassador in Berlin whether a personal letter from Chamberlain or a personal visit by General Ironside would be more effective in convincing Hitler that the British were not bluffing.[66]

Meanwhile, Gladwyn Jebb, one of the ablest younger members on Lord Halifax's staff, was entertaining the German chargé d'affaires, Dr Theo Kordt, at his home on the evening of 18 August (evidently, the source of some of Halifax's information in the letter to the Prime Minister). Kordt, assisted by 'several old brandies', assured Jebb that there would be no war 'either because the Poles would be terrified into submission or because the English would let their Polish allies down'.[67] Jebb notes that he had the impression that Dr Kordt, 'as a good German, was convinced of the necessity, if not of a war with Poland, at any rate of a display of power designed to bring Poland permanently into the German orbit'. Kordt showed no sign whatever, Jebb adds, that the German government would

[64] Feiling, p. 416.

[65] DBFP, vol. VII, p. 81.

[66] But as will be seen from Slessor's account and the *Ironside Diaries* as well as from the official history, this is what the British were doing with regard to the Polish issue – and Hitler had no doubts about it.

[67] DBFP, vol. VII, p. 555.

be prepared to compromise. 'I must say he seemed in the last resort reconciled to a world war over Poland if Germany's will was opposed by other Powers,' Jebb concluded. Jebb added also his own assessment: his instinct told him that Hitler would not risk a world war on the Polish issue 'at this particular moment'.

That weekend, Hitler and Stalin reconciled their immediate differences and by Tuesday morning, 22 August, the news of their impending Pact had reached the British and French governments. Sir Samuel Hoare noted the pained surprise of the Cabinet's Foreign Policy Committee when they were told. Henderson had assured them that there was no substance in rumours that such an agreement was brewing, and Seeds, the British Ambassador in Moscow, had been kept 'completely in the dark'.[68] Chamberlain called a Cabinet meeting for that Tuesday afternoon, 22 August.[69]

Before going to Downing Street, Hore-Belisha, the Minister for War, lunched with his three senior generals, Gort, Ironside and Pownall. Belisha was worried and asked Ironside for more information about the Polish situation. The news from Moscow had depressed Belisha; he felt that the British were in a bad way. Ironside urged him to demand the mobilization of the Regular and Territorial Armies when the Cabinet met.[70]

The request was put to the Cabinet by the Defence Minister, Lord Chatfield, but Chamberlain opposed the additional call-up affecting some 110,000 men.[71] It was a curious situation. The Chief of the Imperial General Staff, Lord Gort, had taken no formal stand.[72] The Secretary for War, Hore-Belisha, wrote to the Prime Minister immediately after the Cabinet meeting, bargaining for sixty thousand to be called up, if not the 110,000;[73] otherwise, he said, it would take a week to mobilize

[68] Templewood, p. 360.

[69] Hore-Belisha's diary wrongly gives the date of this meeting as 23 August; see *Belisha Papers*, p. 217.

[70] *Ironside Diaries*, p. 89.   [71] *Belisha Papers*, p. 218.   [72] *Ironside Diaries*, p. 89.

[73] On 26 August, Hore-Belisha received permission to mobilize 35,000 men, *Belisha Papers*, p. 221.

in an emergency with the attendant risk of congestion if it coincided with evacuation and air raids.[74]

Chamberlain explained that mobilization at this time would be misunderstood by Hitler and might interfere with the appeal which he proposed to make on the following Thursday in a speech in Parliament. He also intended to send a personal letter to Hitler which would set out Britain's determination to stand by her obligations to Poland which had not been in any way qualified by the proposed German Pact with the Soviet Union; but the government remained of the opinion that there was nothing in the difficulties that had arisen between Germany and Poland to justify the use of force, which would inevitably result in a European war. After the Cabinet meeting, a communiqué was issued stating this fact and also that the government would ask Parliament for Emergency Powers on the following Thursday, and that certain precautionary measures had been authorized. After the meeting the Chiefs of Staff issued instructions to all commands that should air attacks on Germany become necessary they were to be directed only against targets conforming strictly to the narrow interpretation of 'military objectives'.[75]

What Chamberlain had not told the Cabinet – neither Hore-Belisha nor his military advisers had any knowledge of it – was that on the day before, 21 August, the Foreign Secretary had received a message from Germany suggesting that Goering would like to come to London to see Chamberlain. Most secret arrangements were made at once for Goering to arrive on the Wednesday – 23 August – the day after the Cabinet meeting. He was to land 'at a deserted aerodrome' and then be taken by car to Chequers. There the staff would be given the day off and the telephone would be disconnected while the Chamberlain–Goering talks proceeded.

Chamberlain and Halifax waited all day on Tuesday for confirmation of Goering's impending arrival – and this was

[74] ibid., p. 218.
[75] *Strategy*, p. 11 and p. 567; also Slessor, p. 213.

probably the real reason for Chamberlain's unwillingness to authorize the mobilization of the Regulars and Territorials which Chatfield and Hore-Belisha had requested. But no confirmation came. On Thursday morning, before Parliament met to pass the Emergency Powers' Bill, Halifax received a message to the effect that Hitler had vetoed the visit because he did not think 'it would be immediately helpful'.[76]

But the interlude had served Hitler's purpose; whether by accident or design we cannot tell with certainty. It had reinforced British hesitation and delayed the kind of action that Hitler feared most. Even on that Thursday morning, after the Goering visit had been called off, when the Cabinet met at lunchtime before Chamberlain went to the House of Commons, the Prime Minister was still unwilling to authorize any measures that indicated British determination to act at once if the Poles were attacked. He told the Cabinet that they had met not to take decisions but to be informed of the latest developments.[77] He also advised them that the British Ambassador in Berlin had reported Hitler as saying that if there were any further mobilization measures in Britain, the German armed forces would be fully mobilized 'as a protection and not a threat'. Chamberlain still resisted any further substantial call-up that might thus provoke Hitler. He wanted to wait until after Henderson had seen Hitler that day.

So far, therefore, Hitler – the prisoner of his timetable – had been more successful in keeping the British becalmed than the French. Admittedly, French mobilization was under way and the French army was a far greater immediate military threat to the Germans than were the British, but Hitler was convinced that the French would not move without British political and military support. Therefore, the important thing for him was to ensure that the British remained undecided and inactive to the last possible moment. Thus, when he finally told the British that Goering was not coming, there were less than forty-eight

[76] *Halifax*, p. 444.
[77] *Belisha Papers*, p. 219.

hours to go before the time scheduled for his armies to march into Poland. When Chamberlain told his Cabinet that day that they had not come to take decisions, that was all that Hitler could have hoped for; for without British decisions there would be no French action on the western front.

We can see now the full implication of the failure by all concerned – the intelligence services, the German resistance, the 'well-informed' diplomats – to appreciate the full significance of the decisions taken by Hitler at his small conference at Obersalzberg on 14 August. For they made nonsense of the diplomatic and political charade that followed. The military decisions had been finalized; the timetable was set; the rest was camouflage, and eminently successful as we can see.

We must turn back here to 22 August. While the service chiefs were lunching with their Minister at the Carlton in Haymarket,[78] and speculating about the Nazi–Soviet deal, and while at Downing Street the Prime Minister and his Foreign Secretary were secretly and expectantly awaiting confirmation of Goering's impending arrival, Hitler had called a grand conference of all his commanders in the conference room at his home in Obersalzberg. They met – like Belisha and his generals – at noon on 22 August. Goering was there, at Berchtesgaden, not preparing for a meeting with Chamberlain; he was receiving his final battle orders.[79]

There have been three or four different versions of what Hitler said at this briefing; there are some discrepancies between them on details but not on the substance of Hitler's introductory outline of his intentions and plans. It is difficult, therefore, to accept the claim by General von Manstein that both he and General von Rundstedt left Berchtesgaden with the conviction that there would be no war, that the Poles would submit and

[78] See p. 10 above.

[79] Earlier that morning, Goering had a private briefing, which he had requested, from the Chief of Staff, General Halder, to coordinate measures between the Luftwaffe and the army; see Halder, pp. 22–3.

that neither the British nor the French would take the risk of embarking on a possible world war.[80]

The notes which the Chief of Staff, General Franz Halder, made of Hitler's two speeches emphasized the military parts of his briefing: that it was necessary to free Germany's rear in the east before she had her final showdown with the West; that it was desirable for the Wehrmacht to be tested before the decisive battle. Germany had to be firm, Hitler told them, the counter-moves by Britain and France would come. They had to act with unqualified ruthlessness. The aim was not to establish a new and better frontier – it was to destroy the enemy – Poland, in the first instance. The date for the attack was set for 26 August.[81]

Admiral Boehm made rather fuller notes than Halder, and so did General Warlimont, Jodl's deputy at the Fuehrer's headquarters. Boehm's version quotes Hitler in greater detail, explaining that he had taken the decision in the spring to bring about this confrontation. He had assumed that he would have to act first against the West before turning on Poland. But circumstances had compelled him to reverse the priorities. He had reached the conclusion that if he attacked France and Britain first, the Poles would launch an offensive against the German rear while he would be fully occupied in the west. But neither the French nor the British would attack the West-wall while he was engaged in settling Germany's score with the Poles. British rearmament was not real, largely propaganda. 'We shall hold the West until we have finished with the Poles.'

A further compelling reason for not delaying action was the unfavourable development of Goering's Four Year Plan. The restrictions would begin to tell in another few years; they were far better placed for action in 1939 than in 1942 or 1943. The risk which they had to recognize and had to take was that Britain and France would strike at Germany in the west. The

[80] Manstein, p. 21.
[81] Halder, pp. 24–6.

fact was that they had no choice: they had a good chance of winning now because of the Anglo-French inaction; they had no chance of winning the war in another few years.

In the second session, Hitler was more specific about the immediate situation. He again urged his commanders to be ruthless, firm and unsentimental. Speed was everything. He advised them that the attack would take place in all probability on Saturday morning – in four days' time.[82] When Hitler had finished, Goering led the applause and thanked the Fuehrer on behalf of all present for his magnificent leadership. He also expressed their absolute determination to see that his wishes were carried out.[83]

No time was wasted. That evening, von Weizsaecker at the Foreign Ministry received the detailed plan from the German representative at Danzig, von Veesenmayer, of the manner in which the Poles were to be provoked to take action which the Germans could consider as *casus belli*. He described how stores of weapons which were to be discovered had been planted, and detailed the five stages that would follow in order to produce the necessary crisis:[84] the Poles would be compelled to take such measures as would justify Germany's resort to force. Veesenmayer asked that the message be passed on urgently to the Fuehrer.

It was. Next day, when the British Ambassador came with Chamberlain's personal letter, Hitler wound up his long talk with Henderson with the warning that at the next Polish provocation, he would act. 'The question of Danzig and of the Corridor will be liquidated, *so oder so*. I want you to take note of this.'[85] But the message was seen in London only as yet another counter in the bargaining for position – and Hitler may well have meant it as a means of intimidating the weak British Cabinet. In fact, it did not matter to him very much,

[82] DGFP, vol. VII, pp. 167–72.
[83] ibid.
[84] ibid., p. 155.
[85] ibid., p. 180.

so oder so: he was sure now that the British would not act when he marched. Everything else was for the time being irrelevant. That afternoon he had authorized the Wehrmacht to launch the attack on Poland on the morning of 26 August: three days to go.

But all was not yet settled – or lost. For one fleeting moment that evening while Hitler was laying down the law to the British Ambassador, the initiative passed to the French. France's Council of War met at the War Ministry in Paris, on that Wednesday 23 August, with the Prime Minister, Daladier, in the chair.[86] Also present were the Foreign Minister, the Air and Navy Ministers, the members of the General Staff – Gamelin, Darlan, Vuillemin, Jacomet and their principal assistants. Daladier put three questions to the Council, the three questions which the British and French governments had been duty bound to have answered months ago. But here was a last – the last – opportunity. Daladier asked the Council to provide him with the answers:

'1 Can France accept the disappearance of either Poland or
   Rumania, or of both, from the European scene?
'2 What possibilities are there to oppose this development?
'3 What measures must we take now?'

The discussion on the first question centred on General Gamelin's military assessment. He and Admiral Darlan emphasized the importance of ensuring Italian neutrality, but they evaded the specific Polish issue. Gamelin suggested that there might be no need for immediate action. He believed that the Polish forces 'would resist honourably' and so prevent the Germans from turning against France before the following spring. By that time, Gamelin added, France would have the assistance of the British forces.

After a good deal of discussion, Foreign Minister Bonnet argued that in view of the German-Soviet Pact it would be wiser not to enter into war now but to wait for a more opportune

[86] Georges Bonnet, *La Défence de la Paix*, vol. II, p. 305 et seq.

time. This was not the consensus of the Council. It agreed that France would have to meet her obligations to the Poles. These were not affected by the abortive Anglo-French negotiations in Moscow.[87]

The Council then turned to consider the second question: what could they do to prevent the destruction of Poland and, possibly, Rumania? The Air Minister, La Chambre, said that France was equipped with large numbers of modern fighter planes which, together with those of the British, would match those of the Germans and Italians. They would not have a substantial bomber force until 1940. Until then the British would take responsibility for the massive bombing of Northern Germany.

La Chambre then turned to the German Air Force. It had 12,000 planes available[88] but he did not think that this should affect the decision of the government. No one challenged his information and no one believed in his assurance that the French Air Force could match a force of such numbers. The discussion turned to the possible consequences on French civilian morale once the German air attacks began. This, clearly, was the thought uppermost in the mind of the participants.

General Gamelin and Admiral Darlan, in turn, considered the action possible by the land and sea forces of France. Gamelin said that the army was in a state of readiness. It could, however,

---

[87] It is not without significance or irony that on the day before – on 22 August – the French leader of the negotiating team in Moscow, General Doumenc, prepared a draft Anglo-French-Soviet Military Agreement for presentation to the Russians that evening. Because of the announcement of the Pact with Germany it was never presented. But Article 3 of the proposed agreement, and to which the French and British governments had given their approval, read as follows: 'Should the attacker turn against Poland and Rumania ... France and Britain will immediately operate with all their forces against the attacker.' – see D B F P, vol. VII, p. 605; see also Slessor, p. 214: 'the vague term "all support in our power" really meant nothing because it was not in our power to give any support.'

[88] We know now that the Germans had only 3,600 planes of which 2,600 were on the Polish front, close on a thousand were allotted to defence of the Reich and only very few as a token support for the western front.

do little at first against the Italians (whose neutrality had been all but assured by Foreign Minister Bonnet earlier in the meeting). Gamelin added that they could give no direct aid to the Poles, but the French mobilization would be of some relief to them as it would draw a considerable number of German troops away from the Polish front. In conclusion of the debate on this question, Premier Daladier reminded the participants that since France would be called upon to fight alone for some months, they had to safeguard the security which their defensive system on the frontier provided.

There remained only the third question, what to do now? It turned on purely domestic measures: security precautions and steps to anticipate a possible outbreak of war – the precautionary mobilization in good time. This, in fact, was already under way. It was all that was necessary, that and the realization that the French were the masters – that they had the Germans at their mercy once the Wehrmacht began to move against Poland. But after an hour and a half, Daladier closed the discussion. The French decided not to exercise their option. At the Wehrmacht Headquarters, General Halder met that day with Keitel and the Chiefs of Staff of the Luftwaffe and the Fleet. They fixed the time for the attack on Poland for Saturday morning at either 4.15 or 4.30.[89] In London, Chamberlain and Halifax were still waiting for Goering's peace mission.[90]

[89] Halder, p. 27.
[90] *Halifax*, p. 444.

5

Evasive Action

The fatal act was not Hitler's decision to destroy Poland and to go to war against Britain and France at the first opportune moment; these decisions had been taken much earlier. The time for the destruction of Poland had been set as long ago as April; the decision and timing for the challenging of the Anglo-French hegemony in Europe came later in the spring. Therefore, as far as Hitler was concerned, the last week of August – once the Soviet Pact was in the bag – mattered only in connection with the technical details of launching the war against Poland and keeping the British and French from actively intervening in it. That there would be war was no longer a matter for discussion. Short of complete Polish submission there was nothing that could prevent it.[1]

The fatal decision was that of the British and French governments. They continued to believe – though with noticeably decreasing conviction – that strong words and firm postures would deter Hitler from going to war. They had never accepted – not even after Hitler's occupation of Prague in March – that, short of complete submission, Hitler was intent on war. They had never grasped – as Churchill did – that there no longer was a deterrent short of war that would halt Hitler in his tracks; that the only way of preventing him from gaining complete mastery over Europe, was to ensure his defeat in war. The French and the British had the means and opportunity, as

[1] Halder, p. 46; *Keitel*, p. 214.

we have seen, during these last weeks of August to decide on action that would have led to Hitler's defeat that autumn. They refused even to consider its possibility. Why?

On the morning of 25 August, with barely twenty four hours to go before the Wehrmacht was to launch its concerted attack on Poland, the British Chiefs of Staff met at the War Office to continue their discussion of the night before on the implications of the Soviet-German Pact. The general tenor was that there would be no war, and the betting odds offered by the senior officers reflected this conviction. The Chief of the Imperial General Staff, Lord Gort, offered five to four against an outbreak of war; his deputy, General Sir Ronald Adam, gave slightly better odds against war – six to four. Only General Ironside was certain that there would be war; he laid five to one on war.[2]

The Cabinet did not meet that day, but Halifax signed the Anglo-Polish (Mutual Assistance) Treaty. Chamberlain was waiting for the arrival of Henderson with Hitler's reply to his letter. At the same time, a reasonably accurate summary arrived from the British embassy in Berlin of what Hitler had said to his commanders at Obersalzberg on 22 August: a further clear indication of his intentions. Meanwhile, however, Hitler had called off the invasion of Poland at the last possible moment after hearing that the British had concluded a treaty with Poland and that Italy had decided to remain neutral in case of war.[3]

Henderson arrived in London on the morning of 26 August, a Saturday. The Cabinet met that evening with Henderson in attendance. Chamberlain's draft reply to Hitler's message was thought to be 'too fulsome' by the War Minister, Hore-Belisha and by Kingsley Wood, the Air Minister. Chamberlain agreed to toughen some of his formulations. Belisha again raised the question of mobilizing the Territorial Field Army. It would mean calling up around 300,000 men. Henderson was asked

[2] *Business of War*, p. 13.
[3] *Keitel*, pp. 210–12.

what, in his opinion, would be Hitler's reaction to such a step. Henderson replied that it might make the difference between Peace and War. Chamberlain took the hint. He authorized Belisha to call up 35,000 Territorials so as to relieve the militia at vulnerable points.[4]

In Berlin at the Reichs Chancellery there was great confusion throughout 25 and 26 August.[5] Hitler's hesitations and last-minute stop on the attack on Poland had produced much critical reaction in the armed forces, but it turned out to be little more than the customary soldiers' grumbles – even though many officers joined the critics. It never reached the dimensions which some of the principal resistance officers imagined. Oster was convinced that Hitler could not survive such a setback; he was sure that Hitler had become the laughing stock of the armed forces. Oster's principal, Admiral Canaris, the head of the German counter-espionage service, who with Oster was the main link with Allied intelligence, agreed with him. Both were certain that British firmness on 25 August, as demonstrated in the signing of the Polish Pact, had paid off. Hitler would not now risk a war which would embroil him with the British.[6] One cannot help wondering whether this confident interpretation of the situation was the basis for General Gort's certainty that there would be no war. Until that morning, moreover, the War Office had received no report of general mobilization in Germany.[7]

But no sooner had Henderson left the Chancellery on 25 August, to report to Chamberlain, than Hitler and his advisers proceeded to consider the next step. He had earlier said to Keitel that he had wanted 'more time to negotiate'.[8] But Hitler understood that whatever else he had, it was not time. 1 September was his deadline. His letters to London and Paris,

---

[4] *Belisha Papers*, pp. 220–1, but Belisha's dates and details must be treated with caution; they are frequently incorrect.

[5] *Keitel*, pp. 212–3.

[6] Gisevius, p. 370; Gert Buchheit, *Ludwig Beck*, p. 214.

[7] *Ironside Diaries*, p. 90.

[8] *Keitel*, pp. 212–13.

E

his 'feelers' through Goering, and through other channels, had successfully reassured the British. He did not fear their language, only their bombers and their fleet – and the French army allied to Britain. Within hours of Henderson's departure with the Fuehrer's reply to Chamberlain, Hitler had fixed a new time for the attack on Poland, 31 August.[9] In the event it was to be postponed once more, but only once more, to 1 September.

It was only now, moreover, that the German High Command realized the full measure of the risk that Hitler proposed to take on the western front. He cut their troop allocations far beyond their stated minimum requirements. Every soldier, every gun, every tank and every plane that could be spared was to go east. The officers were appalled. Hitler was serenely confident that neither the British nor the French governments and their military advisers would make any rash move to aid the Poles. He had hesitated for a brief moment on 25 August; but now he was certain. He had reason to be.

In London, the members of the Imperial General Staff appeared to be of little use to the government which was wracked by indecision, fear and ignorance, and beset by a total lack of political understanding for the issues that were at stake, or of the nature of the Hitler régime. For the men who were in command of Britain's armed forces were, with only a few exceptions, in much the same state as the politicians. Rarely in a crisis have military men been so little in command of the situation as the Chiefs of Staff of Britain and France during the last week of August. They had the means but they had neither the mind nor the will to act.

The nightmare which had haunted Hitler and the German generals had been the prospect of having to fight a war on two fronts. It was one immense advantage of which Hitler could not rob the French and the British once they were allied with the Poles. Admittedly, he had averted the danger during the Czechoslovakian crisis in 1938; he had successfully bluffed his

[9] ibid.

way through that, but he could not do the same again to the British and the French. He had, therefore, surprised them with the Soviet Pact, but even this did not save him from the threat of a war on two fronts: the Russians would on no account risk embroilment in a war with Britain and France.

This, then, was the central theme which one might think would have preoccupied the Joint Anglo-French Planning Staff from their first meeting in March to the last. But the record is blank. If the matter was discussed at any time, it was quickly scotched. It never reached the Committee of Imperial Defence. The concept of exploiting German weakness at no stage reached either Cabinet level or the more restricted Foreign Policy Committee of the Cabinet.[10]

We have seen how at earlier meetings of the Joint Staffs and the Committee of Imperial Defence there was a defeatist trend about any immediate action, no matter what. Now, at the height of the crisis, in the middle of August, the Committee was informed that the decision to increase the initial expeditionary force from two divisions to four 'had resulted in a shortage which meant that hardly a unit went to France completely equipped.' The representative of the War Office advised members that the position was so bad that they would not be able to equip their thirty-two divisions before 1942.

In fact, this was largely irrelevant at the time. The one question which one would have expected to be put – and

---

[10] This is not altogether surprising when we consider the views of some of those who shaped the thinking about defence. We have the evidence of Marshal of the Royal Air Force, Lord Douglas, who was the deputy chief of the air staff at the time. He writes in his memoirs that during the time that he had spent at the Imperial Defence College with Alan Brooke and Admiral Ramsay 'we never discussed, in our work as instructors, what might be called the principles or the theory of war; and we did not waste our time on any high-falutin' pretensions about theory. To us the object of war was to win it quickly and as economically as possible.' – see Douglas, p. 43; Slessor sent a personal memorandum to the Chief of the Air Staff in which he urged that the Poles should be told that they would get no help from Britain and France. In fact, he added, the Germans had no cause to fear a war on two fronts since the British and French were in no position to do anything worthwhile, see Slessor, p. 230.

answered – did not materialize. At least at the French Council of War they asked the right questions, even if they did not answer them. In London, neither the General Staff nor the government posed the question bluntly: what aid would be given to the Poles? No one expected much from the Army; but there was the RAF and there was the Navy.

The Royal Air Force capitulated even before the question was put. In case they got the wrong idea, the Germans were told on 22 August, that there would be no air attacks on German cities, only on rigorously controlled military targets. Bomber Command was said to be an investment for the future which ought not to be frittered away by operations against minor targets.[11] RAF attacks would be confined to the German Fleet and to the dropping of propaganda leaflets over the Reich. But this information was withheld from the Poles.

It was a strange situation. The French army was mobilized and ready for action. The British Navy had been alerted and was at sea. The RAF had an impressive – under those conditions – hard core of a strategic bomber force (something which Germany lacked). British aircraft could attack Northern Germany and the Ruhr. A formidable force thus stood poised for action. But its leaders and commanders had neither the plans nor the will that would have effectively set this great force in motion. Instead they turned to the diplomatic side-show with which Hitler sought to distract them until he was ready to strike.

Seen against the hard reality of the gathering of German armies and the overwhelming Anglo-French superiority in the west, the diplomatic exchanges provide a peculiarly vivid illustration of what happens when diplomacy and power become separated from each other.

On the morning of 25 August, Sir George Ogilvie-Forbes, the British Minister in Berlin, sent a personal letter to Ivone Kirkpatrick of the German department at the Foreign Office. He enclosed a summary of the speech which Hitler had made

[11] *Strategic Air Offensive*, pp. 134 and 137; *Strategy*, pp. 17, 20, 567.

to his commanders at Berchtesgaden on 22 August. The ambassador had seen the report but was too busy to take it with him to
London. Therefore, says Ogilvie-Forbes in his letter, he is
sending it to Kirkpatrick 'for your private eye and such disposal
as is fitting'. In this manner, information which might well have
been a most significant element in the decisions which the
Cabinet was about to take, was relegated to a private letter
and lost from all further official attention. Instead of appreciat-
ing this further confirmation that Hitler had taken the plunge
into war, instead of mobilizing for swift action, the Cabinets in
London and Paris continued to dally, and the soldiers and the
diplomats continued to doubt Hitler's intention to risk a world
war.

Birger Dahlerus, Goering's Swedish intermediary, reported
on 27 August, after delivering a letter from Lord Halifax, the
Foreign Secretary, to Goering, that he was now convinced that
Hitler and Goering wanted peace. He was not the only one to
draw hasty conclusions.

In Whitehall, the Foreign Office's specialist on Germany,
Ivone Kirkpatrick, wrote a 'Minute' that same day,[12] 27 August,
in which he came to the conclusion that 'the fact that Herr
Hitler regards the Secretary of State's message to Field Marshal
Goering as satisfactory and is quite content to hold his hand
shows that the German Government is wobbling'. Kirkpatrick
found that his view had been confirmed by a member of the
German embassy, presumably Theo Kordt, with whom he
was in constant contact. Kirkpatrick considered therefore that
the British government should be conciliatory in form but
absolutely firm in substance. The latest indications were, wrote
Kirkpatrick, 'that we have an unexpectedly strong hand'. The
news from Turkey and Italy was most satisfactory. The 'dubious
Russian assistance' would not compensate Hitler for Mussolini's
failure to march.

The 'Minute' was shown to Halifax. He expressed full
agreement and said that he had these considerations constantly

[12] DBFP, vol. VII, pp. 314-5.

in mind.[13] One cannot but wonder whether by this time Kirkpatrick had read Ogilvie-Forbes' letter and the summary of Hitler's briefing of the commanders. If he did, as we must assume, then he evidently paid no attention to it; nor, it seems, did anyone else.

The gap between the diplomatic dreamworld and the military realities was widening with every passing hour. While Kirkpatrick was speculating on Hitler's intention and advising a firm stance, Sir George Ogilvie-Forbes, who was in charge of the British embassy during Henderson's absence in London, and the French Ambassador Coulondre were exchanging notes on the telephone – with the German *Abwehr* listening in. A report of their conversation went to the Chief of Staff, General Halder,[14] and he noted that 'our opponents know that we had intended to invade Poland on 26 August'; the enemy also knew, Halder noted, the new date set for the attack, 31 August. General Halder also learnt from the intercepted conversation of the two diplomats that Henderson was to play for time when he came back. Here we are again confronted by this curious puzzle: the British chargé d'affaires in Berlin was accurately informed of the German intention to launch the attack on Poland; so was the French Ambassador. But there was no evidence of this certainty either in London or in Paris. Far from it.

Henderson was due to see Hitler late the following evening, after ten o'clock. Earlier in the afternoon Hitler had another meeting with Halder, Himmler, Wolff, Goebbels and Bormann.[15] He told them that he was determined to achieve a settlement: either Danzig was handed over to them, and their other demands met, or they would proceed ruthlessly. In fact, by the time Hitler spoke with his inner circle the last option had gone. Just after three o'clock that afternoon the order had gone out from General von Brauchitsch, the Supreme Commander

[13] ibid., vol. VII, p. 315.
[14] Halder, p. 38.
[15] ibid.

of the Army, setting the time for the postponed invasion of
Poland. Zero hour was to be early on 1 September.[16]

These times and decisions are significant for the appreciation
of the revealing part played by the diplomats. Thus at 3.22 that
afternoon of 28 August, the order to march was again given
from Hitler's Reichs Chancellery. At 5.30 Hitler met with his
military and SS advisers and told them of his general intentions
to go ahead and step up his demands on Poland 'according to
the military situation'.[17] At 10.30 Henderson came with
Chamberlain's message. Hitler read it and then settled down to a
serious discussion about possible ways of consolidating Anglo-
German friendship, and Ribbentrop wanted to know whether
Chamberlain would carry the country for such a policy.
Henderson reassured him. Hitler asked whether 'England
would be willing to accept an alliance with Germany', and
Henderson replied, 'speaking personally', that he did not
exclude such a possibility. The conversation ended shortly
before midnight with the promise by Hitler that he would reply
in writing by the following day. Henderson said there was no
hurry, he was 'quite prepared to wait'. But not Hitler: he
replied significantly that there was no time to wait.[18] Henderson
returned to the embassy and sent a full report of the meeting in
the early hours of the morning of 29 August.

One would have thought that on that Monday morning the
central factor for consideration at the Foreign Office and at the
Quai d'Orsay was that Poland and Germany were mobilized;
that France had completed her extensive pre-mobilization and
that the date set for the launching of the invasion of Poland was
(at that time) barely forty-eight hours away – and that Hitler
had told Henderson during the night that 'there was no time to
wait'. The signals could hardly have been set more visibly. But
there was one topic that found no place that day on the agenda
of either the British and French governments or on that of the

16 ibid.
17 ibid.
18 DBFP, vol. VII, p. 353.

General Staffs of the two countries: now that the assault on Poland was imminent, what were they going to do? What, in fact, were they going to tell the Poles? Nothing was said on either count.

Judging by the intellectual preoccupation of the Foreign Office that day, one must conclude that the Kirkpatrick interpretations still prevailed. Henderson's report of his talk with Hitler did not spark off the final preparations for confronting the now inevitable attack on Poland in the most effective way possible; it started a subtle discussion on the best way of formulating an agreement with Hitler.

It was opened with yet another 'Minute' by Kirkpatrick.[19] Hitler had two courses open to him, he noted. He could go to war, in which case there was no need for any more discussion. But Kirkpatrick evidently thought that Hitler would take the second course, and this worried him. He warned his superiors that Hitler might reduce his demands to an acceptable level. In that case he would have fulfilled his promise to recover Danzig without shedding blood. He would also have secured an 'implicit British promise to restore colonies and to come to an understanding with Germany.' The important thing, therefore, argued Kirkpatrick, was not to abandon hope of peace. 'If we are wise and firm' a tolerable *modus vivendi* could be achieved on this basis – even possibly a measure of disarmament.

Kirkpatrick's 'Minutes' so intrigued the Permanent Under-Secretary, Sir Orme Sargent, that he added one of his own. He feared that Hitler might have a third course open to him: that he was in a position to exact a settlement on his terms by threatening to break off the negotiations. These two comments brought forth a third, from the Foreign Secretary himself.[20]

Lord Halifax minuted on 30 August that there was reality in the anxieties mentioned by Kirkpatrick – 'a settlement without war by abatement of Hitler's demands' or in Sir Orme Sargent's third possibility of a bad settlement under the threat of breaking

[19] ibid., vol. VII, p. 354.
[20] ibid.

off negotiations. 'We must be on guard for both contingencies,' noted the Foreign Secretary. And then we get one of those revealing insights into Lord Halifax's thinking on the eve of the war. 'It may be,' he writes, 'that no settlement is possible so long as the Nazi régime remains in control of Germany. But I don't think that ought to be conclusive in favour of not working for a peaceful solution on proper terms now. And when we speak of Munich,' Halifax continued 'we must remember the change that has supervened since then in the attitude and strength of this country . . .' Halifax concludes from this that 'if Hitler is led to accept a moderate solution now, it is perhaps not altogether wishful thinking to believe that his position will suffer a certain diminution of prestige within Germany'.[21]

The Cabinet met the same day to consider Hitler's reply. The discussion centred almost entirely on the diplomatic prospects of a settlement and the terms on which this might be negotiated. Belisha intervened at one stage with the information that the Germans had deployed forty-six divisions against Poland and fifteen against the West but not even this roused the members to consider the strategic implications of an outbreak of war. The sad fact was that by now the Poles had been written off as a military factor in the equation of peace and war.[22] It made no difference to allied planning whether they fought or not, whether they held out for three months or for three weeks. Neither the RAF nor the French Army would be affected by it. They had made their plans independently of the Poles. They were not going to provoke the Germans by any kind of aggressive action on land or in the air. In a sense, therefore, the military side of the Polish question was settled even before the war broke out, *so oder so*, as Hitler would have said. What remained were the diplomatic possibilities which continued to engage the British and French long after they had ceased to have any reality.

[21] ibid.
[22] This emerges clearly from the official history as in *Strategy*, and is described vividly by Slessor, p. 231.

While Halifax had speculated in his 'Minute', and while the Cabinet had devoted another session that Tuesday to the discussion of the terms of a settlement, Hitler had given the order for the attack to begin at 4.30 in the morning of Thursday. Himmler had already distributed lists with names of those to be arrested by his secret police, the S D. These were so numerous and the measures contemplated were so ruthless that both Goering and Halder questioned their advisability.[23] In the discussion at headquarters and in the Chancellery it was noted that Britain was 'soft' towards taking warlike action,[24] and would not intervene.[25]

This 'impression' – for it was hardly more than that – was received with considerable relief, for German mobilization was proceeding much slower than had been anticipated. There were more than the anticipated difficulties. The Westwall was far from finished when von Leeb reported that day that the remaining labour force working on the fortifications was disintegrating – a third of them had been called up, another third had run away, and the rest were evidently ineffective.[26] Moreover, army units were no real substitute for constructive workers. The last thing the German High Command wanted under such conditions was a French attack on the Siegfried Line or British air raids on the demoralized fortification workers. They had nothing to fear.

Gamelin continued to advise the French and British to do nothing to provoke German retaliation;[27] the Imperial General Staff urged that the Poles and the French be advised to take no 'impetuous' actions which might result in German air attacks on Britain and France.[28] The air forces of both countries had already decided to reduce their possible targets so as to virtually eliminate themselves as an active factor in the war against

[23] Halder, p. 44.
[24] ibid., p. 43.
[25] ibid., p. 49.
[26] ibid., p. 47.
[27] *Strategic Air Offensive*, vol. I, p. 137.
[28] *Strategy*, pp. 56–7.

Germany during the opening weeks that mattered so much. Hitler appeared to be the only man in the picture. When he wrote to Mussolini on 26 August,[29] he was able to give him a vivid and accurate description of the state of mind in London and Paris. He would proceed to defeat Poland, 'even at the risk of complications in the west', but neither Britain nor France would do anything decisive before the war in the east was settled. Then in the winter or the spring he would turn on them with adequate forces at his disposal.[30] However, the British and French governments and General Staffs continued to grope in ignorance and with false hope of still avoiding a war which they could have won there and then.

In the early hours of 1 September, according to plan, the German armies invaded Poland. There was no formal declaration of war, but rarely could the opponents of an aggressor have had more adequate notice of his intentions. The Poles had mobilized rather late in the day, largely because of British pressure not to do so 'prematurely' in order not to provoke the Germans. The attack caught them, therefore, partly unprepared with mobilization still proceeding. French mobilization had been under way for some days and, contrary to so much that was written later by way of apologia, the French First Line troops were in a greater state of readiness than any others of the armies involved – including the Germans.

But the most important thing that had happened as the Germans crossed the Polish frontier was the collapse of the British policy of deterrence. The government, the diplomats and the armed forces had staked everything on their conviction that Hitler would be deterred from attacking Poland by the British threat of a resultant world war. At 4.30 a.m. on Thursday 1 September, Hitler marched undeterred into Poland. Neither the British nor the French were prepared for their next move *in military terms*. They were not even ready with the political alternative of a declaration of war. On the contrary, it is evident

[29] Kirkpatrick, p. 404.
[30] ibid.

now that had Hitler played the political card which Kirkpatrick and Orme Sargent had feared so much in their 'Minute' of 29 August,[31] he could have obtained almost his maximum demands without further fighting. But Hitler decided on war, and his generals waited with mounting incredulity as nothing happened on the western front.[32]

The Poles were also getting anxious. Nothing which they had been told during the many discussions with the British and French had prepared them for such appalling passivity. And not even then, on the first days, did they realize that this was considered policy and not simply the delays of the war machine in motion. The first inkling came when the French Ambassador in Warsaw, Léon Noël, called on Colonel Beck, the Prime Minister, after the German attack had been under way for over twelve hours to tell him of Mussolini's attempt to call a conference to settle the Polish question peacefully. Beck replied, with evident justification, that as a result of an unprovoked attack, Poland was in the midst of a full-scale war. 'This is not a matter for a conference but of resisting the attack through the combined action of Poland and her allies.' Beck added that air attacks had been continuous since morning and there had been considerable casualties.[33]

In London, the Polish Ambassador went to 10 Downing Street where he met the Foreign Secretary. He gave Halifax more details of the German attack and asked whether Britain's pledge to Poland would now become operative. Halifax recalls that he told the Ambassador that 'if the facts were as stated, I had no doubt that we should have no difficulty in deciding that our guarantee must at once come into force'. There was still no suggestion of hedging, no inkling that what was in the Prime Minister's mind was a long war which would lead not so much to an Allied victory as to an eventual collapse of Germany from

[31] See above, p. 128.
[32] Keitel, Westphal, Manstein, Jodl and Witzleben have written or spoken about their amazement.
[33] *French 'Yellow Book'*, Document No. 343.

internal strain.[34] There was no hint of the conclusion arrived at by the Service Chiefs that Britain would be able to give no material military aid to Poland, that neither the Army nor the Air Force would be in a position to act for another three years, and that the Fleet was too valuable and vulnerable to be exposed prematurely. In Paris it was much the same.[35]

Nothing had been said about such indirect – and delayed – aid in the terms of the British guarantee, in the French discussions or in the Mutual Assistance Pact, signed on 25 August, less than a week earlier. This last had stated categorically that in case of aggression by a European Power (which was defined as meaning Germany) 'the other Contracting Party *will at once* give the Contracting Party engaged in hostilities all the support and assistance in its power'. This was Article One of the Pact. The point was still further emphasized in Article Five where it stated that such mutual support and assistance would be given '*immediately* on the outbreak of hostilities' (my italics – J.K.).

It was therefore neither surprising nor unreasonable that the Poles should expect both swift diplomatic and military response once they were under attack. As we know, there was neither the one nor the other. But the question does arise – and has never been resolved – of whose advice caused the Polish Pact to be signed, particularly in view of the previous argument by the Chiefs of Staff that 'it would be difficult to afford any serious relief to the Poles without, on the one hand, drawing retaliation in more dangerous degree on the Allies' own cities and industries and, on the other, risking the alienation of neutral opinion'.[36]

Looked at more closely it was a very curious conclusion for a Chiefs of Staff recommendation to the Cabinet. For implicit

[34] See Chamberlain's letter to his sister, in Feiling, p. 418: '. . . what I hope for is not a military victory – I very much doubt the feasibility of that – but a collapse of the German home front. For that it is necessary to convince the Germans that they cannot win . . . On this theory we must weigh every action in the light of its probable effect on German mentality. I hope myself we shall not start to bomb their munition centres and objectives in towns . . .'

[35] Bonnet, pp. 272–3.

[36] *Strategy*, pp. 56–7.

in it is the statement that 'serious relief to the Poles' was possible provided the government was prepared to engage the Germans in the air, and provided it could convince neutral opinion – especially the United States – of the rightness of its actions. One must express some wonder in any case at the authority or propriety of the Chiefs of Staff in advising on public opinion in the neutral countries. In any case, one would have thought that this was a risk worth taking, if it meant bringing help to the hard-pressed Poles and striking at the depleted German air and ground forces on the western front.

The Poles also addressed urgent appeals to the government in Paris. On 4 September, a Franco-Polish Mutual Assistance Pact was signed. It was identical with the British prototype. It came into force at once and the Polish Ambassador in Paris requested immediately afterwards that a general offensive be launched in the west on the lines agreed upon by General Gamelin with the French War Minister on 19 May.[37]

On that day, the British Chief of Staff, General Ironside, and the Chief of the Air Staff, Air Chief Marshal Newall, were at Vincennes for talks with the French General Staff. For all the numerous meetings of the Joint Staff Committee which had been held since the end of March, the British Chiefs of Staff could not tell the Cabinet what the French proposed to do under present conditions. Nor had the British told the French what they intended. There was no coordinated action prepared for this eventuality and no combined plan to help the Poles. Nor did the discussions in Paris take the matter much further – certainly not for the Poles.[38]

Ironside and Newall reported next day to the Cabinet that Gamelin intended, after his armies had completed their concentration, to 'lean against the Siegfried Line' around 17 September and test its strength. A breakthrough was possible, they thought, but 'Gamelin had no intention of risking precious divisions in a precipitate assault on so fortified a position'. The

[37] Bonnet, pp. 272–3.
[38] *Strategy*, pp. 59–60; but the best account is in Slessor, pp. 242–4.

Cabinet took note of Gamelin's plan and agreed that British bombers might be used to exploit any break through the German Siegfried Line.

General Gamelin's version of what took place during these Anglo-French discussions puts a rather different emphasis on the British position. He says[39] that on the eve of the meeting with Ironside and Newall, he asked the Chief of the French Air Staff, General Vuillemin, how he proposed to give assistance to the Poles. Vuillemin had replied that 'he had thought' of starting bombing operations on the Polish front 'but for that it was necessary to have the agreement of the British'. We may, for the moment, set aside our wonder at what the French had been discussing with the British all these months on the Anglo-French Joint Staff Committee and turn again to the Anglo-French encounter on the following day, 4 September, to the meeting of General Ironside and Air Chief Marshal Newall with the French General Staff, as Gamelin observed it.[40]

It appeared a rather inconclusive affair. Nothing was settled. Ironside did most of the talking on the British side while Newall was demonstratively reserved about any possible R A F action to relieve the Poles. It seems to have been another typical meeting of the Joint Staffs, only on a somewhat more elevated level.

Two days later, on 6 September, General Vuillemin informed the French General Staff that Polish requests for assistance by the Allied air forces 'were becoming increasingly desperate' while the British response remained firmly non-committal. Vuillemin thought that the opportunity for sending such assistance had gone, certainly for the French Air Force whose equipment was not as good as that of the British. The areas into which bombers would have to be flown were being overrun by the Germans. At this point Gamelin said how right he had been in May when he had refused to commit himself to provide the Poles with assistance from the air should they be attacked. He discussed the same question later with the French Prime

[39] Gamelin, vol. III, p. 50.
[40] ibid.

Minister. Daladier agreed that France could do nothing either by air or by sea to assist the Poles. But surely, he asked, the British with their modern bombers could do something? General Vuillemin explained some of the technical difficulties that faced the British. Gamelin added that in any case, 'the RAF had refused categorically to send aircraft to Poland when it had been requested to do so'.[41]

There were two other, rather more revealing encounters, on that 4 September, when Ironside and Newall were in Paris. The French Foreign Minister, Bonnet, informed General Gamelin that the Treaty of Alliance with Poland had been signed and that the military agreement which Gamelin had reached with the Polish War Minister on 19 May had therefore become legally effective and France was therefore bound to open a second front against the Germans 'with the bulk of her forces'. The Polish Ambassador, Lukasiewicz had made this request to Bonnet immediately after the Treaty had been signed that day. Bonnet records that Gamelin was evasive.[42] He claimed that the agreement had been invalidated because there had been no parallel political agreement at the time of the signature, and he claimed also that he had qualified his undertaking to come to the assistance of the Poles by launching an attack with the 'bulk of his forces', against the Siegfried Line.

Bonnet, who had been a notable appeaser and had done all he could to avoid going to war, was now cast in the position of devil's advocate. He went to see Daladier to impress on him that the declaration of war had changed everything. They must mount a 'violent offensive' to force Germany to fight on two fronts. Poland 'with its eighty divisions'[43] was indispensable to

[41] Gamelin, vol. III, p. 51; Air Chief Marshal Sir Philip Joubert, who was spokesman for Bomber Command at the height of its power, claims in his memoirs that 'it was the pusillanimity of the French Government in 1939 that enforced restraint on our bomber forces which otherwise might have started the first lessons in the general theory that war does not pay'; see his *The Third Service*, p. 118.

[42] Bonnet, p. 272.

[43] ibid.

an Allied victory; what mattered was that 'we did not leave her to be overrun by the Germans in a matter of days'.[44]

Bonnet reminded Daladier that it was because of this need to preserve the Polish divisions for a war on two fronts that General Gamelin had declared himself in favour of going to war at a meeting of the War Council on 27 August. But Gamelin prevailed over Bonnet; so did the RAF. There was no aid forthcoming for the Poles, either on land or in the air.

The speciousness of General Gamelin's excuses, the fact that the Polish government was assured of immediate aid by the French – and by Gamelin himself – and demonstration that the Polish General Staff was never clearly told that there would be no aid from the west if Poland was attacked, were all confirmed when the Germans, after the occupation of Paris, found the text of a letter which General Gamelin had sent to the Polish Commander-in-Chief, Marshal Smigly-Rydz.

It was written on 10 September, and addressed to the Polish Military Attaché in Paris, for communication to the Marshal. It was evidently in answer to a Polish inquiry as to when they could expect effective help from the French? Gamelin replied that more than half his 'active' divisions in the north-east were already engaged in battle. Since they had crossed the German frontier they had been met with firm resistance, 'but we have nevertheless advanced'. Unfortunately, Gamelin added, they were forced into positional warfare because of the defensive capac ty of the enemy, and because 'I do not yet have the necessary artillery at my disposal'.[45] In the air, the French Commander-in-Chief lied,[46] 'we have engaged our air force in conjunction with our land offensive and are conscious of being opposed by a substantial part of the Luftwaffe'. All this was evidence, Gamelin concluded, that 'I have kept my promise to

[44] ibid.

[45] Gamelin had, in fact, something like an eight to one superiority in artillery; see Halder, p. 7; Liss, pp. 88 and 267–70.

[46] In talks with the British, 'General Gamelin thought the less the bombing that took place the better would be the prospects of a French victory in the spring of 1940'. – see *Strategic Air Offensive*, p. 137.

F

attack with the bulk of my forces on the fifteenth day after
mobilization ahead of the time scheduled. It was impossible to
do more.'[47] Two days later, on 12 September, Gamelin, following a meeting with Chamberlain and Daladier, issued orders
to General Georges to halt even the limited offensive actions
against the Siegfried Line on which he was engaged, and to
withdraw his forward troops.[48] In his letter to Smigly-Rydz
Gamelin thus admits to an unqualified undertaking in which
the Poles had put their trust. They had similar promises from the
British and they had therefore embarked on the defence of their
country confident that they would not have to fight alone,
without aid and without relief of any kind from their powerful
western allies.

This was Poland's tragedy; but there was an even bigger one.
The failure to exploit the situation at the beginning of the war
not only left Poland in the lurch, it also forced the world into
five years of destructive warfare. For the military issue in
September 1939 was not whether a western offensive could help
the Poles but whether it would defeat Hitler. At Hitler's headquarters, the generals could not understand what had happened
to the French and the British. Their inaction was 'inexplicable'
to the Germans unless the Allies had 'grossly over-estimated' the
strength of the German forces in the west.[49] It was counter to
all fundamentals of military thinking that the Allies should
permit the destruction of the Polish forces and do nothing while
the Germans were fully occupied in the east. Perhaps, mused
Keitel, Hitler was right: the Western Powers would probably
not continue the war once Poland was defeated. There was no
other answer possible for their otherwise inexplicable conduct.[50]
For every military consideration favoured a violent Anglo-
French counter-offensive in the west.

[47] The text of the letter is printed in Manstein, p. 34. [48] Liss, p. 111. [49] *Keitel*,
p. 216. [50] *Keitel*, p. 216; for considerable evidence of a British promise not
to attack in the West, made during secret talks in which the Pope acted as
intermediary and in which the British Ambassador, Mr F. G. Osborne,
participated in September 1939 see Kurt Sendtner's detailed account of the
'Roman Peace Talks' in *Politik und Zeitgeschichte*, BX/55, 9.3.55.

6

'Operation Waterloo' –
The Battle That Did Not Happen

General Ulrich Liss, the able German officer who had to make a special study of the French forces before and after the outbreak of the war, has rightly warned against judging the fighting capacity of the French soldier in the summer of 1939 by what happened in the summer of 1940, after Poland had been overrun and after a demoralizing year spent in inexplicable inactivity in the trenches and the fortifications of the Maginot Line. The assessment by German intelligence of the French Army on the eve of the war was that it was, as in the first world war, the most dangerous of all possible opponents.[1] The estimate of the sound morale of the French Army was confirmed by General Lenclud at the Riom Trial when he told the court that whenever French troops were engaged against the Germans in 1939 'their morale was excellent'; this was particularly true in the Forbach sector.[2] Generals Blanchard, Mittelhauser and Gerodias gave evidence to the same effect. They also stressed the demoralizing effect of the inactivity during the winter in the field.[3]

French equipment on land was much superior in quality and, of course, in quantity to that of the Germans in the west. The French tank ought not to be measured against later models but by the standards prevailing in 1939. Even a year later, during the invasion of France and after the breakthrough at Sedan, the German armour avoided frontal engagement with either French tanks or the very effective French 25 mm anti-tank

[1] Liss, p. 50.   [2] Tissier, p. 31.   [3] ibid.

gun.[4] The Germans were horrified when they tested this gun after they had overrun France and found that its shell could penetrate even the German Mark IV tanks, not to speak of the bulk of their armour made up of Mark I and Mark II models.[5]

It has also been argued – especially by British spokesmen and particularly by Captain Sir Basil Liddell Hart – that the French army organization was so frozen to static warfare that it was incapable of any sizeable offensive action against the Germans in September 1939. Moreover they accepted, rather uncritically, Gamelin's explanation that the French army required seventeen days to mobilize and that therefore it could do nothing before 17 September – and then it was too late. Neither of these arguments will stand the test of critical examination, as we shall see.

As far back as June and July 1938, at the time of the maturing Czechoslovak crisis, General Gamelin had issued a series of detailed 'Directives' which hinged on a planned counter-offensive against the Siegfried Line between the Rhine and the Moselle, with holding actions on the Upper Rhine and on the Luxemburg sector.[6] There was nothing unduly static in this plan even if it did not conform to the later concept of Blitz warfare. In fact, it could have been applied with great effect against the bulk of the German forces which were concentrated precariously into the Saar front. Gamelin went still further when he submitted a plan to the French government on 1 September 1939 – the day the Germans invaded Poland – which proposed that the most effective way to bring immediate help to Poland would be to attack the Germans in the west through Belgium, Luxemburg and Holland.[7]

One may well ask whether this plan ought not to have been considered more fully by the Joint Anglo-French Staff when

[4] See the evidence of Major Ragaine, Commander of 35th armoured battalion at Riom; Tissier, p. 56; and Liss, p. 100.

[5] Liss, p. 100.

[6] Gamelin, vol. III, pp. 26–32 gives the full text of the Directive of 8 June, and pp. 18–26 give the texts of later Directives issued during July.

[7] ibid., p. 15.

they still had time to consider its political implications – and prepare for them in view of the known Belgian and Dutch opposition to anything of the kind. One might also ask whether the plan had been considered and rejected out of hand because of the Belgian attitude. Such evidence of the Staff talks as is available suggests that the matter came up for discussion but was given no serious consideration because of the political issues involved. What concerns us here, however, is that on 1 September 1939, the French Commander-in-Chief still thought it possible – militarily – to move his forces through Belgium if the political conditions were to permit it. It does not suggest a total inability to launch a counter-offensive under given circumstances. It does not justify the conclusion that the French army could not have taken a violent offensive against the Germans had the political and military will to do so existed in London and in Paris.

The second unjustified assumption of the 'Liddell Hart School' was that the French could not have mobilized in time to take effective action.[8] Much of this view, as we have said, is based on Gamelin's excuse that he needed seventeen days from the day of mobilization which he, later, counted as from 1 September. This was neither correct nor justified.

It will be seen now why we paid such careful attention to the French mobilization dates. The pre-mobilization began, in fact, on 21 August. Moreover, a considerable part of the French fortification and frontier troops had been in position for some time before mobilization. Documents found by the Germans when they took over in Paris showed that the main part of the French mobilization had been completed by 4 September, and that the French Army could then have gone into action. By 10 September, the French were ready with their full complement of armour and artillery – with everything in fact, except the intention to strike.[9]

The French had mobilized 110 divisions, apart from the

---

[8] See Liddell Hart's privately circulated *Notes on the Second World War*, p. 5.
[9] Liss, pp. 88, 111.

General Reserve, the Pyrenean and Coastal Defence, the Navy, the Levant and the Colonial Forces. After making allowance for the protection of the border with Italy and leaving fourteen divisions in North Africa, General Gamelin had eighty-five fully trained and equipped divisions to confront the German Army of von Leeb with its eleven active divisions, supported by another twenty-five incomplete, largely untrained and inadequately equipped second line, Home Guard and replacement divisions.[10] Gamelin had six times more guns than the Germans; he had 1,600 guns apart from his divisional artillery against the Germans' 300 – and the French guns were better and of heavier calibre.[11] Gamelin had some 35,000 active officers serving with his troops; the Germans had less than ten thousand.[12] Gamelin had 3,286 tanks; the Germans had none.[13] The French and British combined had 934 serviceable fighter planes, the Germans had virtually none on the western front; the British had 776 serviceable bombers, the Germans virtually none in the west.[14]

In the central sector between the Rhine and Moselle – where Gamelin had planned his major attack in 1938 – the French had forty divisions in position at the completion of mobilization on 4 September.[15] The Germans were still in the process of assembling their forces, seventeen active divisions with supporting troops of little value, and the French contingent was growing daily.

Had Gamelin executed his plan, it is the opinion of every senior German officer on that front that he would not only have broken through into the heart of Germany, in the direction of Mainz, but he would have trapped the hard core of the German army in the 'sack' in which it had been placed on the Saar Front. One need not speculate on the consequences of this

10 Gamelin, vol. III, pp. 34–6.
11 Halder, vol. I, p. 7.
12 Daladier at Riom Trial; see Tissier, p. 26.
13 Liss, p. 269.
14 Tissier, p. 63.
15 Gamelin, vol. III, pp. 34–6.

action on the war against the Poles; it is sufficient to say that the whole of western Germany would have been wide open to invasion. It would probably have encouraged the generals to act against Hitler and it would have discouraged the Russians from prematurely committing themselves to so uncertain a Nazi ally.

Generals Halder, Keitel, von Leeb, Witzleben, Westphal and Manstein have all worked out possible offensives by which the German lines could have been overrun. But we can confine ourselves to the plan which the French General Staff had prepared but which was apparently never seriously considered by either the British or French governments or by their General Staffs. General Georges, who commanded the vital French sector in the north-east, had reported on 4 September that his troops were in position and ready for the offensive.[16]

The British government and Chiefs of Staff for their part were no more thinking in terms of immediate action, or exploiting the opportunities presented by the German preoccupation, than were the French. The RAF was most anxious to do nothing that would interrupt its planned growth, 'to fritter away resources on minor objectives', as it put it. But no one appears to have suggested the major objective on which the bomber capacity might have been directed – except, that is, Air Commodore Slessor. Bomber Command was seen by the Air Staff as, above all, in need of conservation and expansion; this was rated as second only to the need to avert defeat.[17]

As a result, 'the British were content to carry into effect a policy of restricted bombing' which it was claimed had been approved by the French, while the Wehrmacht turned to crush Poland.[18] Moreover, the RAF reported that since the Luftwaffe had only attacked military targets in Poland, 'Bomber Command would confine its activity to attacks on the German

---

[16] G. Roton, *Années Cruciales*, p. 64 *et seq.*
[17] *Strategic Air Offensive*, p. 134.
[18] ibid.

Fleet and the spreading of propaganda leaflets over Germany.'[19]
This assumption that the Luftwaffe was aiming only at military
targets (Warsaw was one of them) which the RAF and the
Army had advanced against those who wanted Bomber Command to intervene actively against Germany, was rejected by
some highly placed RAF officers.

Air Commodore Slessor, Director of Plans on the Air Staff
and a member of the Anglo-French Joint Staff Committee since
its inception in March, questioned the wisdom of this policy
in a memorandum to the Chief of the Air Staff, prepared during
the first week of the war.[20] The opportunity to attack Germany
while she was engaged on another front was being sacrificed by
adhering to the accepted policy of conservation, Slessor argued:

> 'Although our numerical strength in the air is a most important
> factor, it should not be allowed to obscure other important consider-
> ations. We are now at war with a nation that possesses an imposing
> façade of armed might, but which, behind that façade, is politically
> rotten, weak in financial and economic resources, and already heavily
> engaged on another front . . . At present we have the initiative. If we
> seize it now we may gain important results; if we lose it by waiting
> we shall probably lose far more than we gain.'[21]

It was a perceptive – almost prophetic – warning about which
Sir John Slessor is curiously silent in his memoirs.

Slessor's assessment at the time was shared by the Assistant
Chief of the Air Staff, Air Vice-Marshal W. S. Douglas. In his
memoirs, Lord Douglas describes how events had turned out
to be quite different from their anticipations.[22] Instead of being
allowed 'to get on with the war', the RAF was held back. He
believed then, as he evidently does now, that the British
government was mistaken. The RAF should have been instructed to begin its attack on Germany at once. Instead, the
Germans were allowed to dictate British policy and action.

[19] ibid., p. 135.
[20] D. of Plans Memo, 7 September 1939; see *Strategic Air Offensive*, pp. 135–6.
[21] *Strategic Air Offensive*, pp. 35–6.
[22] Douglas, p. 49.

Douglas and the Air Staff felt intensely bitter over the frustration and humiliation of seeing Poland destroyed without lifting a finger. They felt that the only possible explanation was that the Prime Minister and the Cabinet were still thinking that they might come to terms with Hitler after he had destroyed Poland.[23]

There was, however, another possible explanation. The advice which the British and French Chiefs of Staff had tendered since they had begun their joint consultations had been such as to discourage any government from taking firm action. As we have seen, the government's military, air and naval advisers had said all along that they were in no position to give any aid to Poland or to strike any measurable blow against Germany. Yet, even leaving out the very special case of the Fleet, there can be no evading the conclusion that an Anglo-French counter-offensive on a massive scale (under 1939 conditions) was possible and would almost certainly have been successful. The British and French General Staffs have therefore to share a grave responsibility with their governments in failing to launch the battle that might have won and decided the second world war in September 1939.[24] The opportunity passed, never to return.

[23] ibid., p. 50.
[24] The Poles had at the outbreak of the war 300,000 men under arms; and they had a further 50,000 officers and two million soldiers as trained reserve (see Gamelin, vol. III, pp. 34–6). They were abandoned as a military factor by the British and French General Staffs as of no account in the balance of power.

7

The Lesson of September –
'To Think Like a Fish!'

There was no single action, no single person and no single specific policy that can be held responsible for the failure of the British and French to win and finish the war against Hitler in the autumn of 1939. Men made mistakes; they still do. Men were driven by good intentions and high moral considerations into a course of action which brought disaster to their own and other people. And men in power, in Britain and in France, stooped to the deception of their own people, even their own Cabinet colleagues and their Polish ally, not because they wanted to betray Poland, but because they believed quite honestly that by these means, however questionable, they would be able to deter Hitler from war. But, in the end, they betrayed the Poles because of their own fear of what the Luftwaffe could do to the cities of France and Britain. This belief and fear were based on and justified by the information which was available at the time to the British and French governments and to their advisers.

It is the nature and source of this information, and the interpretation which was placed on it, that needs to be scrutinized most carefully before we close this inquiry into this decisive battle that was never fought. But it is necessary also to consider other contributory factors in the non-decision making of 1939, and in the shaping of the intelligence available to *all* the governments – for in the final analysis the greatest blunder was that committed by Hitler and by his acquiescent German generals who were quite prepared to go along with the Fuehrer so long as only Poland was at stake.

Political attitudes and assessments were more often than not based on social prejudices and preconceptions, and conditioned by a pre-war society still strongly compartmentalized in self-contained groups moulded by the class structure of Britain and France, and by the hierarchical military and National Socialist society of the Germany of 1939. Not even great social upheavals such as the General Strike of 1926 produced class emotion of the intensity and bitterness recorded in the year before the outbreak of the war.

The concept of National Socialist Germany as a bulwark against the spread of Russian communism was far more widely accepted among the ruling and upper classes of Britain and western Europe than can easily be understood by a new generation thirty years later. In most cases, it was not sympathy or support for the racial policies and ideas of the Nazis and Fascists that led to the condonation of Nazi actions and to the lack of resistance among the democracies, in short, to the policies of appeasement; these stemmed in most cases from a fear of spreading Russian influence, exercised through the Popular Front of Léon Blum and the Republican régime in the Spanish civil war, as well as through the more customary communist channels.[1]

Chamberlain recorded his 'most profound distrust of Russia' and his distrust in her motives[2] within a matter of ten days after Hitler marched into Prague; and for the next six months he continued, in his private letters, to express his deepest conviction that Hitler wanted a settlement with Britain and did not seek war.[3] Chamberlain's biographer rightly stressed that this was not altogether due to prejudice; it was based, he claimed, on the intelligence and information which was made available to

[1] An earlier example of this Bolshevik-phobia can be found in the private and secret papers of the British administration in Palestine now in possession of the Israel State Archives.

[2] Feiling, p. 403.

[3] ibid., pp. 416–7.

Chamberlain about the state of the Russian régime and its armed forces – and, presumably, also on the information about Germany and Hitler's intentions.

Neville Chamberlain was no exception. On the contrary, he was one of the most typical men of his time and his class, and of the politicians and soldiers who had charge of affairs during these pre-war months. Their views were surprisingly uniform, with only the hated black sheep marching out of step with their class – a Churchill, Macmillan, Nicolson and a very few others. Nicolson's diaries[4] reveal the extent of feeling which this act of desertion of their class produced among the majority of the Conservative Party; and the private notes of Tom Jones, Lord Lothian, and Ironside show that these men were neither villains nor fools but simply part of a severely restricted society, living within its own horizons, and operating with frozen political and strategic concepts, encouraged by unsuspecting German propagandists who often had no intention of doing Hitler's work, and were unaware that they were doing so. The combination of these factors with diplomatic and military intelligence collected and interpreted by men of their own class and outlook provided the basis for the strategic concept on which the British and French (and, curiously, also Hitler) grounded the fateful policies that were to lead to September.

The British and French governments, and their General Staffs were convinced by their own inclinations (and by their diplomatic and intelligence information) that Hitler would shrink back from risking a world war as a consequence of further local aggression; they believed that their strong words and confidential diplomatic messages, combined with treaties of mutual assistance, would act as an adequate deterrent – if one was necessary. (They were not even fully convinced about Hitler's warlike intentions.) Similarly, Hitler believed (with some justification after Munich) that the British and French would not risk a world war and the threatened destruction of

---

[4] Harold Nicolson, *Diaries and Letters, 1930–1939*; see particularly pp. 356–84.

their cities by the Luftwaffe for the sake of Poland's integrity, in which neither country had vital interests at stake.

Both sides calculated wrongly. Both based their calculation, in part at least, on information received through the usual diplomatic and military channels. Both were, to a considerable extent, bluffing. The British had no intention in 1939 of giving immediate aid to the Poles as soon as they were attacked; nor had the French. The German bluff was in a sense a far more dangerous one for Hitler: he did not have the means, either in the air or on land, to support his threats against the British and the French. They had – in fact – the upper hand during September; as Churchill said, they were the masters. The respective deterrents, however, failed to deter, although both the Allies and the Germans believed in their military reality: the British and French feared the striking power of the Luftwaffe, and the Germans knew that the French hundred divisions were no myth and no bluff. Where both sides went wrong was in the psychological assessment of the possibility that the enemy was prepared to risk a world war. However, both Hitler and the British–French alliance were prepared to do that – even if both had curious and dubious after-thoughts about it. What matters here is that they decided to risk a world war, and that there was no effective alarm bell in operation to warn any of the governments concerned – British, French or German – of this one factor that mattered more than anything else.

Millions of words, confidential and most secret information, the dispatches and gossip of diplomats, military details and economic assessments passed through the intelligence apparatus (in all its aspects) to the decision-makers in London, Paris, Berlin, Rome and Warsaw. What did they know when the hour of decision struck? We have seen the fog of ignorance, mis-information and misjudgement in which they moved. And, therefore, we ought now to look more closely at this 'apparatus' on which Chamberlain, Daladier, Hitler and Mussolini – and the Poles – relied for their guidance. What, in fact, was the 'intelligence apparatus', military and diplomatic, in the summer of 1939?

It was a curious hotch-potch and it ranged widely. In Britain, it was controlled by the head of the Secret Service and by the Foreign Secretary. All military, naval and air intelligence was, in the last analysis, under the authority of the Foreign Secretary – at that time, Lord Halifax. Naturally, he was also the controlling figure for all Foreign Office intelligence, that endless stream of telegrams, letters and formal dispatches that flows into the Foreign Office from every one of the British missions abroad, from 'the privileged spies', the ambassadors, as Piggot described them in his *Political Dictionary* in 1794. But there was no central authority to coordinate information, to assess it and check it, and to prepare considered judgements for the use of the Cabinet. It was a casual affair, with amateurs frequently intervening, and with Ministers taking excited action on the basis of unsupported rumours. There was the case of the General Alert of all home defence in March 1939 following the receipt of a rumour that the Germans were about to attack the Fleet. We have seen, on the other hand, the warning given by the senior intelligence officer of the Foreign Office being treated by Sir Alexander Cadogan and the Foreign Secretary with no more consideration than a passing whim.[5]

There is another complication when we come to consider the sources of information in the critical months before the war in 1939. Apart from information received through the secret services, which – incidentally – appeared to figure hardly at all in the decisions of the government or the Chiefs of Staff, the principal channels of information were the dispatches to the Foreign Office, especially from the missions in Berlin, Paris and Warsaw, the reports of the service attachés in these capitals, and the assessments of the Directors of Intelligence of the Navy, the Army and the Air Force. Yet it is doubtful whether air intelligence under Air Vice Marshal R. E. C. Pierse produced anything which could compare in its impact on government

[5] See p. 14 above.

policy with the reports on the Luftwaffe disseminated by the American Colonel Lindbergh.

In a different way, the Director of Naval Intelligence during these months, Rear-Admiral J. A. G. Troup, was closely and openly identified with the fortunes of General Franco in Spain; he had made no secret of his distaste for the Popular Front in France or anything emanating from the Soviet Union. Captain Liddell Hart has described how he met Admiral Troup at a dinner party and heard him hold forth, in the presence of foreign diplomats, on the extent to which he sympathized with General Franco. 'Knowing how much the Government relied on Admiralty information, I was the more aghast that it should be filtered through such a prejudiced channel.'[6]

This apparent – and real – ignorance about the planned actions of Hitler, and the failure to obtain essential information, is all the more strange in view of the situation in Germany. For there our agents had to contend with men who were, by all accounts, more opposed to National Socialism and Fascism than were some of their British and French opposite numbers. Throughout these months, the heads of the German *Abwehr* conspired with leading officers in the Wehrmacht to bring about the overthrow of Hitler. They were present at Hitler's briefings of 23 May, 14 August and 22 August. They knew of Hitler's every preparation and step. With this team of disloyal generals and counter-espionage agents to assist them, Allied intelligence and diplomacy failed all down the line to anticipate Hitler's approach to war and the defeat of Poland. It seems inconceivable in view of what we know of Admiral Canaris, Colonel Oster, Hassell and Gisevius, not to mention others, that they failed altogether to communicate vital information about Hitler's plans to the Allies.

We know that Oster informed a senior Dutch intelligence officer of the impending attack on 10 May 1940;[7] we know that

---

[6] Liddell Hart, p. 134.

[7] 'Der Fall Oster', in *Vierteljahrshefte zur Zeitgeschichte*, 1966, vol. I, pp. 33–9.

Denmark and Norway were forewarned through Swiss channels in April that year;[8] and we also know of the intimate contact between these German circles and Allied diplomats and service attachés in Berlin. Yet with such extraordinary advantages, how was it that the Chiefs of Staff, the Foreign Office and the Quai d'Orsay, and both the British and French governments were so completely unprepared for Hitler's course of action, although he had provided at least three detailed previews of his plans which were known to these officers of the *Abwehr*, not to speak of those members of the German Foreign Ministry who were equally opposed to Hitler? They all knew the facts. What happened to them? Were they lost in the pipe-lines of the channels of communication, or were they simply filed away without much second thought? Were they deliberately withheld or did they reach their destination only to be ignored?

These are not idle questions about what might have been in 1939, although there has been since then a radical improvement of the technical and organizational aspects of the British and American Defence Intelligence (as it is now) and of the Secret Services. But there has been no fundamental change in diplomatic or political intelligence. It is not so much that their reports are inadequate. They are often intelligent and sound assessments of the local conditions and prospects but they rarely reach beyond into that area of action in which Hitler specialized, which became the hallmark of 1939 and 1940. It is in this connection that we have to look for the lesson of September 1939, a lesson that remains as applicable in 1968 as it was thirty years earlier.

For when we come to analyse the reports of 1939, those published and those still in the files, we find that we can classify them under three convenient headings:

1 British and French unwillingness to believe that Hitler would do anything that seemed to them so preposterous.

8 See author's *Spying for Peace*, pp. 27–8.

2 Hitler's unwillingness to believe in the preparedness of the British and French to respond to his challenge.

3 Exaggerated estimates of enemy strength led to inactivity when decisive action should and could have been taken, or to the waste and misuse of resources and opportunities in order to face these imagined dangers.

The combination of disbelief in the unexpected and belief in exaggerated estimates of enemy strength continued to play a major role throughout the war in the policy-making of the major governments. It was the decisive element in the swift German occupation of Norway and Denmark in 1940, and in the breach of the French front at Sedan in May of that year. It led to the faulty deployment of the Russian forces by Stalin in June 1941, and to their disastrous retreats in the face of the German advance during the following weeks. The Japanese surprise attack on Pearl Harbor was possible only because of the fundamental disbelief of the Americans in the possibility of such an attack.[9]

After Pearl Harbor the Axis seemed to have lost its ability to launch further surprises against the Allies, except in matters of tactics and in the case of the 'Flying Bombs' directed against the civilian population of London. But as the strategic surprise factor appeared to lessen, the other principal element to which I have referred began to play an even more decisive role – the exaggeration of enemy strength.

It was, however, not a simple form of intelligence exaggeration. It was a far more complex affair; it sprang directly from the circumstances of 1939: from the fear and disinclination to challenge the Germans on land in Europe. As the Germans began to dig in strategically and psychologically, with such terminology as the 'Atlantic Wall' and 'Fortress Europe', they

[9] All the technical and operational failures at Pearl Harbor, which have been so fully investigated and described in Roberta Wohlstetter's *Pearl Harbor*, were the natural consequences of this disbelief, despite considerable evidence that the Japanese were preparing to attack.

began again to feed Allied intelligence with the same kind of recipes that had been so successful in 1938 and 1939.

From 1942 onwards, but especially in 1943, the British and American assessments of German strength on the Atlantic Wall greatly overestimated the numbers of Germans defending the Fortress Europe in the west; Allied planning for an invasion of Europe as a major relief operation for the hard-pressed Russians was repeatedly nullified by the size of the expedition required in the light of the vastly exaggerated intelligence estimates of German defensive strength in the west.

But it was not just that. Linked with gloomy reports of the difficulties involved in overcoming the Germans in the west, were the rosy estimates of Bomber Command and of the American Strategic Air Force. These appeared to provide the substitute for an invasion. They claimed to be destroying the Luftwaffe and the German aircraft industry. They were, in the contemporary words of Air Marshal Harris of Bomber Command,[10] 'dehousing the Germans' in calculated terror raids about which the British press was requested to keep quiet lest British public opinion might protest against these British and American air force methods. It was thus the combination of exaggerated reports of German strength in the west with exaggerated reports of the damage Allied bombers were inflicting on the Germans that contributed substantially to the delays in mounting the invasion of Europe – and in ending the war.

The exaggerations of the German capacity to resist did not end with the Allied landing in Normandy in June 1944. At that time, the German civilian and administrative front in the Rhineland was in a state of total collapse and panic. There was no longer any worthwhile organized defence had General Patton pushed on to the Rhine and beyond in September. The Germans there were waiting to surrender and submit; they could no more understand the Allied hesitation to advance in the autumn of 1944 than they could understand it in September 1939 – five years before. A lot had changed in these years but not the

[10] At an 'off-the-record' briefing of air correspondents of the British press.

bogeys that inhibited the Allied governments and generals from grasping at the opportunity to end the war there and then.

And just as the French and the British Generals, Foch and Haig and the rest, were – in October 1918 – still planning another year of war before Germany could be defeated, so right to the end of the war, the British and Americans feared a grand final stand by the German élite troops in the *'réduit'* of the Bavarian and Austrian Alps. They calculated the Germans would be able to prolong the war for possibly another year or more and so compel the Allies to accept negotiated terms. There was, of course, no real basis for such an assumption, but it achieved a high degree of credibility in the highest Allied quarters.[11]

This habit of exaggerating enemy strength did not end with the war. It has continued to flourish in all its second world war variations. In 1948, British army expectations – expressed most forcibly by the Chief of the Imperial General Staff, Field Marshal Montgomery – were that the Arab armies would overrun the defences of the Jews in Palestine in a matter of days; in 1951 the Americans in Korea were taken by complete surprise when the Chinese crossed the Yalu river.

But in a class by itself was the NATO estimate of post-war Russian strength which dominated the western world's military and political attitudes and policies during the years of the cold war. The Russians were believed to have enjoyed an overwhelming superiority in conventional forces over those deployed by the NATO Powers. For a decade or more, NATO thinking was influenced by this central thought. Later came the American conviction that there was a serious missile gap between American and Russian strength which still further reinforced the Soviet posture of superiority in Europe; this was to play a significant part in Kennedy's presidential election campaign in 1960.

The first substantial crack in these assumptions came during

[11] See Kimche, p. 151 and also a thorough investigation of this myth by R. G. Minott, *The Fortress that Never Was.*

the Cuban missile crisis in October 1962 when Kruschev's assumption that the Americans would not risk a nuclear world war over the Cuban missiles, was similar to that of Hitler in 1939. Like Hitler, Kruschev had mistakenly assumed that his opponent would shrink back from the prospect of a world war, but the consequences were less dire because, unlike Hitler, Kruschev had the sense and the courage to draw back while there was time when he found that he had been wrong.

It was only after this Cuban experience that the American and British intelligence organizations began to review their existing information on Soviet strength. They reached the startling conclusion that they had not only been wrong but that the situation was precisely the reverse of that which had been generally accepted. It was NATO that enjoyed substantial superiority over the Russians, not the other way round. The West was superior to the Russians on land, in the air and at sea; the West was also substantially stronger in the nuclear arms race. All these years, it was realized, the Russians had been far more afraid of the West than the West had been of the Russians. One might therefore excuse the Soviet leaders for believing that the Western leaders had deliberately exaggerated Soviet strength so as to provide a pretext for attack. Again, as in 1939, neither the diplomatic nor intelligence assessment and communication was such as to provide a timely corrective for the wrong appraisals in Washington, London and Moscow.[12]

The Vietnam miscalculations are of too recent origin to require further elaboration; they serve, however, to emphasize that the basic conditions for such errors have not been changed materially by the technological, mechanical and personal improvements that have been made in the collection of diplomatic and secret information. But the problem comes nearer to the heart of the real difficulties of our time when we come to consider the Chinese puzzle. In the case of China, and also of

---

[12] A detailed analysis of this affair was given by the Defence Correspondent of *The Times* (now Lord Chalfont) on 12 August 1963, and by Jon Kimche in the *Sunday Telegraph* on 6 October 1963.

Burma and the Islamic world, the collection and communication of both formal diplomatic and secret intelligence information – in both directions – is confronted by a wide gap of totally differing civilizations, by unchartered and unpredictable historical processes and methods of thinking, by outlooks and aspirations which move on entirely different levels to those accepted and customary in the West.

This greatly adds to the possibilities of surprise action, of the wholly unexpected taking place. It was this that Hitler had pioneered. He understood the decisive importance of psychological shock and surprise – in war as in politics – and he made the most of his opportunities. His unexpected moves were not necessarily based on secrecy in timing and location. It could just as simply be that the surprise he achieved was to be found in the manner of the action, such as the breakthrough at Sedan in 1940, or the landing on Crete in 1941.

Today, we seek protection against misinformation by all kinds of new technological devices. We have vast and costly organizations to ferret out the intentions of other governments, so as to anticipate them in their possibly hostile intention. They in turn have similar organizations and devices so as to mislead and confuse us, and in order to anticipate our next move. But in the light of the experience of 1939, we may well ask whether these huge and costly machines, ranging from formal diplomacy to the most sophisticated forms of intelligence, can really provide the answers that men have sought ever since Joshua sent spies into Jericho.

There is an old Arab proverb that 'if you want to catch a fish you must think like a fish'. In a world where Americans have to understand the Chinese, and the British have to understand the Russians, the Jews have to fathom the Arabs, and the Indians have to understand the French, and vice versa, the ability to think like a fish is far more important than the analyses fed into the most sophisticated of computers.

For at the end of the road there stands a Chamberlain and a Daladier, a Hitler and a Mussolini; a Halder, a Gort and a

Gamelin. If the costly experience of September 1939 – and nothing in terms of human lives and treasure could have been more expensive – has taught us anything at all, it is that the instruments which modern society has placed at the disposal of its rulers in the making of their decisions were quite inadequate for the purpose. We have the raw material, more than enough. There was no need to dig for more original documentation. What we had to do was read aright that which we had. For it revealed far more than the reasons for the Allied failure during the first twenty days of the second world war.

The lesson of the unfought battle of September 1939 is that modern society cannot afford to rely any longer on the pattern of diplomacy and intelligence evolved during the last century. The foreign and secret services, however modernized in all their technological aspects, have become as outmoded as the biplane – and as dangerous for those who still rely on them. Since there are few secrets in the age of electronic diplomacy that can be effectively preserved, it might be to the general advantage of mankind to establish an International Intelligence Agency which would correct those fearful intelligence conclusions mistakenly arrived at which have been at the root of most recent major wars – and which could easily lead to yet another – and greater – conflict.

Bibliography

This list of books notes only relevant and useful sources. It omits many that were researched as a matter of routine. It also omits the unpublished files of documents at the Public Record Office and the Foreign Office Library which I have consulted and also others which I was permitted to read but not to quote or mention.

I have found in this context that the so-called secondary sources which are treated with disdain by some historians frequently provide more important and significant insights than do many of the unpublished collections of documents which have become something of a modern fetish.

Books are listed alphabetically with the short title used in footnotes given first.

BECK: Gert Buchheit, *Ludwig Beck*, Munich 1964.

BELISHA PAPERS: R. J. Minney, *The Private Papers of Hore-Belisha*, London 1960.

BONNET: Georges Bonnet, *Quai d'Orsay*, Isle of Man 1965.

BULLOCK: Alan Bullock, *Hitler, a study of tyranny*, London 1964.

BURCKHARDT: C. J. Burckhardt, *Meine Danziger Mission*, DTV Dokumente, Munich 1962.

BUSINESS OF WAR: Sir John Kennedy, *The Business of War*, edited with a preface by Bernard Ferguson, London 1957.

CHURCHILL: Winston S. Churchill, *The Second World War*, vol. I, London 1948.

CIANO DIARIES: Malcolm Muggeridge (editor): *The Ciano Diaries, 1939–1943*, London 1947.

COLVIN: Ian Colvin, *Vansittart in Office*, London 1965.

DALTON: Hugh Dalton, *The Fateful Years*, vol. I, London 1957.

DBFP: Documents on British Foreign Policy, 1919–1939, Third Series: vol. IV, January 23–April 3, 1939, London 1951; vol. V, April 4–June 7, 1939, London, 1952; vol. VI, June 8–August 14, 1939, London, 1953; vol. VII, August 15–September 4, 1939, London 1954.

DGFP: Documents on German Foreign Policy, Series D, vol. VI, The Last Months of Peace, March–August 1939, London 1956; vol. VII (German edition, *Akten der Auswaertigen Deutschen Politik*), The Last Weeks before the War, Baden-Baden, 1956.

DIRKSEN PAPERS: Ministry of Foreign Affairs of the USSR, *Documents and Materials Relating to the Eve of the Second World War*, vol. II (*The Dirksen Papers*), Moscow 1948.

DOUGLAS: Sholto Douglas (Lord Douglas of Kirtleside), *Memoirs*, vol. II, *Years of Command*, London 1966.

ELLIS: L. F. Ellis, (*History of the Second World War*), *The War in France and Flanders, 1939–40*, London 1953.

FEILING: Keith Feiling, *The Life of Neville Chamberlain*, London 1946.

FORRESTAL DIARIES: Walter Millis (editor), *The Forrestal Diaries*, New York 1951.

FOUNDING FATHER: Richard J. Whalen, *The Founding Father*, London 1965.

GAMELIN: General M. C. Gamelin, *Servir*, vols. II & III, Paris 1946 and 1947.

GAUCHÉ: General Gauché, *Le Deuxième Bureau au Travail*, Paris 1953.

GISEVIUS: H. B. Gisevius, *To the Bitter End*, London 1948.

HALDER: Franz Halder, *Kriegstagebuch*, vol. I, *14.8.1939–30.4.1940*, Stuttgart 1962.

HALIFAX: The Earl of Birkenhead, *The Life of Lord Halifax*, London 1965.

HASSELL DIARIES: Ulrich von Hassell, *The von Hassell Diaries, 1938–1944*, London 1948.

HENDERSON: N. Henderson, *Failure of a Mission*, London 1940.

HITLER'S TABLE-TALK: H. R. Trevor-Roper (editor), *Hitler's Table-Talk, 1941–1944*, London 1953.

HOSSBACH: Friedrich Hossbach, *Zwischen Wehrmacht und Hitler*, 1934–8, Goettingen 1965.

IRONSIDE DIARIES: R. Macleod and D. Kelly, *The Ironside Diaries, 1937–1940*, London 1962.

JACOBSEN: H. A. Jacobsen, ed., *Dokumente zur Vorgeschichte des Westfeldzuges, 1939–1940*, Goettingen 1956.

JONES: Thomas Jones, *A Diary with Letters, 1931–1950*, London 1954.

JOUBERT: Sir Philip Joubert, *The Third Service*, London 1955.

KEITEL: Walter Goerlitz, *Keitel – Verbrecher oder Offizier*, Goettingen 1961.

KIMCHE: Jon Kimche, *Spying for Peace*, London 1961.

KIRKPATRICK: Sir Ivone Kirkpatrick, *Mussolini*, London 1964.

KLEIN: F. Klein, *Germany's Economic Preparation for War*, Cambridge, Mass. 1959.

KORDT: Erich Kordt, *Nicht aus den Akten*, Stuttgart 1950. See also Kordt's, *Wahn und Wirklichkeit*, Stuttgart 1947.

LIDDELL HART: B. H. Liddell Hart, *Memoirs*, vol. II, London 1965.

LISS: Ulrich Liss, *Westfront 1939–40*, Neckargemuend 1959.

LOSSBERG: General von Lossberg, *Im Wehrmachtfuehrungsstab*, Hamburg 1949.

LOTHIAN: J. R. M. Butler, *Lord Lothian (Philip Kerr)*, London 1960.

MAISKY: Ivan Maisky, *Who Helped Hitler?*, London 1964.

MANSTEIN: Erich von Manstein, *Verlorene Siege*, Bonn 1955; English edition: *Lost Victories*, with a Foreword by Capt. B. H. Liddell Hart, London 1958.

MENDELSSOHN: Peter de Mendelssohn, *Nuremberg Documents*, London 1946.

MILWARD: A. S. Milward, *German Economy at War*, London 1965.

MORGAN: General Sir Frederick Morgan, *Peace and War*, London 1961.

MUELLER-HILLEBRAND: B. Mueller-Hillebrand, *Das Heer*, vol. II, *Die Blitzfeldzuege 1939–41*, Frankfurt am Main 1956.

NAMIER: L. B. Namier, *Diplomatic Prelude, 1938–9*, London 1948. See also Namier's *Europe in Decay, 1936–40*, London 1950; and *In the Nazi Era*, London 1952.

NAZI CONSPIRACY: United States Government Printing Office, *The Nazi Conspiracy of Aggression*, vols. III, VI and VII, Washington 1946.

NEMESIS OF POWER: J. W. Wheeler-Bennett, *The Nemesis of Power, The German Army in Politics: 1918–45*, London 1953. See also same author's *Munich, Prologue to Tragedy*, London 1948.

NICOLSON: Harold Nicolson, *Diaries and Letters, 1930–9*, London 1967.

NOTES ON IRONSIDE DIARIES: B. H. Liddell Hart, *Notes on Ironside Diaries*, privately circulated, London 1962.

NOTES ON THE SECOND WORLD WAR: as above, privately circulated, London 1965.

O'NEILL: Robert J. O'Neill, *The German Army and the Nazi Party, 1933–1939*, London 1966.

OSTER: *Der Fall Oster in Vierteljarhshefte zur Zeitgeschichte*, vol. I, Munich 1966.

PERTINAX: 'Pertinax', *Grave-diggers of France*, New York 1944.

POLISH WHITE BOOK: *Documents concerning Polish-German and Polish-Soviet Relations, 1933-9*, London 1939.

ROBERTSON: E. M. Robertson, *Hitler's Pre-War Policy*, London 1963.

ROTON: G. Roton, *Années Cruciales*, Paris 1947.

SCHLABRENDORFF: F. von Schlabrendorff, *Secret War against Hitler*, London 1966.

SHIRER: William L. Shirer, *The Rise and Fall of the Third Reich*, London 1960.

SLESSOR: Sir John Slessor, *The Central Blue*, London 1956.

SPEARS: Sir Edward L. Spears, *Assignment to Catastrophe*, London 1954.

STEHLIN: Paul Stehlin, *Auftrag in Berlin*, Darmstadt 1965; original edition, *Témoignage pour l'Histoire*, Paris 1964.

STRATEGIC AIR OFFENSIVE: Sir C. Webster and N. Frankland, *The Strategic Air Offensive against Germany, 1939-45*, vol. I, *Preparation*, London 1961.

STRATEGY: J. R. M. Butler, (*History of the Second World War*), *Grand Strategy*, vol. II, September 1939-June 1941, London 1957.

TAYLOR: A. J. P. Taylor, *The Origins of the Second World War*, Fifth Impression with a new introduction, London 1963.

TELFORD TAYLOR: Telford Taylor, *Sword and Swastika*, London 1952.

TEMPLEWOOD: Viscount Templewood (Sir Samuel Hoare), *Nine Troubled Years*, London 1954.

TIMES: History of The Times, vol. IV, pt. II, 1921-1948, London 1952.

TISSIER: Pierre Tissier, *The Riom Trial*, London 1943.

TRIAL OF MAJOR WAR CRIMINALS: *International Military Tribunal*, vols. XV and XX, Nuremberg 1948.

UNITED STATES STATEGIC BOMBING SURVEY: *The effects of the strategic bombing on the German war economy*, Washington 1945.

WARLIMONT: Walter Warlimont, *Im Hauptquartier der deutschen Wehrmacht, 1939-1945*, Frankfurt am Main, 1962.

WEIZSAEKER: Ernst von Weizsaecker, *Erinnerungen*, Munich 1950.

WESTPHAL: Siegfried Westphal, *Heer in Fesseln*, Bonn 1950.

WISKEMANN: Elizabeth Wiskemann, *Rome-Berlin Axis*, Revised Edition, London 1966.

Index